Public Teaching

one kid at a time

Penny Kittle

Foreword by Donald H. Graves

Afterword by Donald M. Murray

Heinemann
Portsmouth, NH

Heinemann
A division of Reed Elsevier Inc.
361 Hanover Street
Portsmouth, NH 03801–3912
www.heinemann.com

Offices and agents throughout the world

The author and publisher wish to thank those who have generously given permission to reprint borrowed material:

"Painting" was first published as "Renewal" in *Classroom Leadership Online* 3 (9), August 2000. Copyright © 2000 by the Association for Supervision and Curriculum Development. Reprinted with permission from ASCD. All rights reserved.
"One for the Road" was originally published in *The Conway Daily Sun,* Conway, NH.

Library of Congress Cataloging-in-Publication Data
Kittle, Penny.
    Public teaching : one kid at a time / Penny Kittle ; foreword by Donald
H. Graves ; afterword by Donald M. Murray.
        p. cm.
    Includes bibliographical references.
    ISBN 0-325-00571-0 (alk. paper)
        1. Kittle, Penny. 2. Teachers—United States—Biography.
    3. Teaching—Anecdotes. I. Title.

LA2317.K557 A3 2003
371.1'0092—dc21
[B]   2002190846

Editor: *Lois Bridges*
Production editor: *Sonja S. Chapman*
Cover design: *Jenny Jensen Greenleaf*
Author photograph: *Parker Forbes*
Compositor: *Drawing Board Studios*
Manufacturing: *Steve Bernier*

Printed in the United States of America on acid-free paper

07 06 05 04 03 DA 1 2 3 4 5

The teachers I love most have grace.
Their work is not proficiency and outcome,
it's poetry and ministry.

—Jonathan Kozol

contents

· · · · · · · ·

foreword

. . . .

I remember the day I first read something by Penny Kittle. It was a classroom vignette, but it was no ordinary piece of writing. In it, Penny described a student attempting to write a personal narrative. Her series of quick, illuminating details allowed me not only to see the student at work but also to sense his life unfolding. I don't ordinarily run into writing of such high quality. I zapped it to my close friend Don Murray, saying, "I think this is pretty good" (I guess I wanted to show some restraint). Murray replied, "It's a lot better than you think. Who is this woman?"

Penny Kittle is an extraordinary teacher who writes. And because she has taught in classrooms ranging from first grade through high school, these short essay–stories show the full range of what it means to teach today.

We live in an era in which measurement is the maxim, scores and standards the norm. Every teacher knows that scores are very narrow and simplistic data. Conversely, it is in the shared story, teacher's and student's, that solutions exist. Stories contain emotional data that open up the head to good, solid instruction. Indeed, it is in the well-chosen story that authors like Penny show the truth about teaching today. Penny goes beyond—way beyond—the numbers to show faces, lives, passions, and very difficult struggles. Best of all, she has the gift of brevity, teaching well in very few words.

Penny lives the maxim, "Everyone has a story to tell." She observes and listens to students young and old. She pushes for their stories whether as essay, poetry, personal narrative, or fiction: she knows the voice is in the story no matter the genre. And she gets stories because she writes stories herself. She exposes herself by writing with her students, asking their help through draft after draft. It is in her own composing that her students learn about the function of writing—to think, to understand, to read differently as authors themselves.

Public Teaching brings you close to the action in today's classrooms. Penny Kittle doesn't duck the difficulties. You will meet three students who eventually drop out of school. You will be surprised by a child who blurts out that her mother died that very morning. And you will laugh at embarrassing moments with adolescents as Penny concludes, "We are their entertainment."

Most important, Penny's stories will remind you that you have your own stories to tell. You will observe the students in your room differently. You will want to write about them, about you, about everything.

—Donald Graves

acknowledgments

In the world of teaching children to write,
all roads lead to Donald Graves.
—Shelley Harwayne

It is, without a doubt, due to the enthusiasm and patience of the Dons that you see this collection of stories in print. When I first stumbled upon *Writing: Teachers and Children at Work* while teaching fifth grade in Knappa, Oregon, I could never have imagined coming to know its author, Don Graves, as a friend and writing companion. Don will sit beside me on his deck and patiently ask questions until I've figured out what it is I have to say. He shares his own writing so I can learn from his process at work. He introduced me to Donald Murray, a man I had read and worshipped from afar, but again, never believed I would meet as a friend. Don has talked me through my writing and given clear, simple ways to make it better. "Get out of the way of your story" is a lesson I continue to learn. Their words are bookends to my work here; they provide the strength it needs to stand.

So many of my colleagues at A. Crosby Kennett Jr./Sr. High School in Conway, New Hampshire, inspire me daily with their courage and their compassion, their professionalism and their dedication. Teachers continue to reach students no matter what the obstacles. I am especially grateful to Karen MacDonald, a close friend and first listener, and Jack Loynd—"O Captain, my Captain!"—the leader of our ship in stormy waters. My writing group friends—Carrie Costello, Dow Villeneuve, Eben Plese, Ed Fayle, Ishi Hayes, Ryan Mahan, Lyon Virostko, and Bonnie Minick—have inspired me often with their own words and talents. Their thoughtful revisions have rescued many of my pieces.

Two different times in my career I stumbled upon a colleague who reshaped my vision of teaching. Renee Harrah and Tamara Chipps are exceptional teachers and lifelong friends. We shared work spaces and coffee and I came away a better teacher. I am grateful.

My dedication to writing began with my students in an eighth-grade language arts classroom in 1999, who shared stories with passion, humor, and love. Those students graduate from Kennett in 2003. I will always remember them seated in our pink-and-white-striped author's chair, reading their work for the class. I thank them for stepping forward with courage, teaching me to risk the truth in my own work. Those students, along with all of the others stretched across five states, are the reason I'm still teaching.

To my editor, Lois Bridges, thank you for making me feel like a writer from the starting line; that's how I got to the finish. Lois is kind and careful with her words, but excellent at rooting out the essential problems in a piece.

My parents began my journey in education by sacrificing much to send me to college. They have read and encouraged my storytelling with warm emails. Thank you Mom, Dad, and my sister, Linda. It is something to live at such a great distance from family, but we stay close and I'm grateful.

Jim Burke, Jennifer Kallmes, and the John Fuller Elementary teachers' writing group read early drafts and offered suggestions as well as high fives. Thank you. I am continually moved by the writing of so many other teachers: Lucy Calkins, Nancie Atwell, Linda Rief, Shelley Harwayne, and Tom Romano, to name a few. Their words have reached across the isolation of this profession and inspired me.

Thank you to Kylene Beers and the editors at *Voices from the Middle*, who published my piece "Writing Giants, Columbine and the Queen of Route 16" in the fall of 2001. Finding a voice in that journal led me to pursue this book.

I've always listened hard to my best friend and husband, Pat. He has brought me breakfast so I could keep writing, fielded phone calls and the requests of our children for months so that I could revise. He has read my work with interest and enthusiasm over and over. He's the first one to tell me that my work with kids matters and I have to keep trying. Our children, Cameron and Hannah, have been patient as I have labored over this book, coming to sit quietly on the couch near my desk or sliding a drawing under the door. My family is the lighthouse I head for in a storm.

introduction

What it takes to be a responsive teacher is not about following a manual, as some outsiders would have us believe.

—Regie Routman

I sank my teeth into a chocolate caramel and savored its sticky sweetness. I was sampling candies at See's, one of my favorite places to be. My son Cameron called from behind me, "You gotta see this T-shirt!" and I cringed. I didn't want to move. I sensed another battle over what was written on the shirt and what I would allow him to wear to school, but he was insistent. He wasn't going away.

We wandered into a store of white and I hastily licked my fingers clean. As I stared at the shirts hanging high above us, a young man approached hesitantly. "Can I help you?" he asked.

"No," I barely noticed him, "we're just looking."

Cameron scowled at me.

"Um, wait. I think I know you," the clerk said, and I turned to examine his short blond hair and kind blue eyes.

"I don't think so," I offered.

"Aren't you Mrs. Kittle?" he asked, hands clasped behind him, a shy grin making me pause.

I smiled. "Yes," and looked closer. He was familiar, almost.

"I'm Keith Johnson. You were my fourth-grade teacher in Long-view," he continued. "You look exactly the same." After thirteen years! I remembered this charming kid. He was a darling little nine-year-old who called me "lemon belly" as my maternity leave drew near. Keith was filled with funny stories and a natural giggle when he was in my class.

"Of course I remember you," I reached out to squeeze his arm, "how are you?"

Cam watched us. "This is my son, Cam, you know, the one I was having that year I was your teacher." We both looked at my grown son, such an obvious mark of the many years that had passed since we'd last met.

"I'm great," he smiled broadly, confident and mature. He went on, "I always wanted to tell you how much I liked the way you taught math. I just graduated from college and with a math major. I chose math because of the way you taught me."

Thank you, Keith.

I don't think my feet touched down for the rest of my vacation that summer in Oregon. I have dreamed of a meeting like this with every one of the hundreds of students I've known over my career. Not all of them would be as kind as Keith, I'm sure, but I long to see them anyway. Some would get an apology for all of the ways I failed them; some, like Steven, who threw up all over me as he struggled to get to the nurse's office, might apologize to me. But the essential truth is this: when you enter teaching you enter the lives of kids. It will change you. There will be days when you realize how lucky you are to know these kids well, and you'll literally spring out of bed, eager to be in your classroom. There will be days when the frustrations and the distrust of the public will break your spirit and tempt you to quit. You will meet kids who are heroic simply because they keep going amidst challenges we can hardly fathom. You will become connected to them in ways I can't explain, and when they move on, you will always miss them. It takes great heart to be a teacher. You have to make room for hundreds of children, because in many ways, they never leave you.

We will only see fragments of our work as the years go by; we'll find students like Keith if we're lucky, but we'll also wrestle with questions that linger long after the children have moved on. Even with the unfair pay, the relentless pressure, and the struggle to make a real difference, I love this work. The kids are worth it. In this book, I make teaching public; I bring you inside my classroom and show you what it has meant in my life to teach.

# of frog legs, crickets, and Superman's cape

The teaching life is filled with the constant need to adapt.

—Donald Graves

I hadn't moved in more than an hour. My body was cemented in place. I lay on my bed waiting for a phone call from Oregon State University. They were sure to call and dismiss me from student teaching. Any minute now. I had tumbled far and fast in one humbling afternoon. I had thought I was a Super Teacher and would instead have to live with the fact that I was human. A failure, but human.

I watched scenes from my classroom replay across the ceiling above. I winced at slimy frog legs with little flipper toes leaping high. I sighed, remembering Hanna's tear-filled resentment as she put on her coat. I finally had a vision of a classroom completely out of control with all the horrid particulars vividly revealed. My classroom. I watched it again, one small mistake compounded by another, leading to that moment when the screams drew teachers from other classrooms and I saw myself screaming as well. In fright, or quite possibly, hysteria.

I was in my final year of college. I was used to studying teaching methods in my education program. This is cooperative learning. See all the students learning from each other? Now you try it. I'd gather with my friends in class to discuss each strategy, comparing it with disdain to the teachers from my past. We were going to be Super Teachers, a new breed. Lying on my bed that afternoon, I studied my own mistakes as a self-satisfied senior in education. *That poor rookie has made all the wrong moves.* I could see my classmates snicker and smirk. *At least*

we can be sure no one would be thick enough to hire her after this.
The tears quivered at the corners of my eyes.

It started when my cooperating teacher poked his head in the room at 2:15 one Friday and said, "Your stuff has arrived from Ohio." I had been teaching solo for three weeks, which was just enough time to feel invincible. I was twenty-one, after all. I glanced at my students quietly working in rows. I paused, considering if I should disturb them.

"Shall I bring them down?" Mr. Hathaway whispered, still perched at the threshold. He knew I had been impatiently awaiting this delivery. His eyes smiled. I hesitated for just a second. Spontaneity is tempting, but I preferred meticulous, cautious planning. It occurred to me that a lot could happen in the remaining forty-five minutes of the school day. Perhaps I should think this through, but Mr. Hathaway seemed eager, and I wanted so much to please him.

"Why not?" I answered. I could handle anything; I was almost sure of it.

Months before, I had been assigned to this fifth-grade classroom by the professors in my elementary education program. I had always been a star student, passionate and thorough. I accumulated As in my coursework like pennies in a jar: one after another. But all education students wait nervously for student teaching. It is the real test. I desperately wanted to ace this experience, but it is one thing to understand the theories, another to make them work. In the three weeks I had practiced my craft in this classroom, very little had gone wrong. One student had almost sliced off his thumb while working on his carving of an apple head before school, but it wasn't my project (blame the art teacher) and I had whisked him to the nurse, one hand firmly on his quaking shoulder, the other staunching the flow of blood with a cloth wound tightly in a fist. I had even remembered to tell the rest of the students to put down their paring knives while I took Kirk to the office. The parents and principal had thanked me for my prompt attention and smooth handling of this difficult situation. Not bad. Super Teacher modestly folds her cape into her jacket and returns to class.

So when Mr. Hathaway came down the hall with a large cardboard box, I gathered my students around a front table and told them our creatures had arrived. There were cheers and scramblings as students reached for science journals and pencils. We had planned carefully for a study of terrarium life. In cooperative groups the students had gathered rocks, moss, plants, and sticks to create an environment for their creatures. Each terrarium had a name: The Moss Pit. Alien Invasion. Grass Valley. The glass cases were neatly lined up against the back wall, waiting. My students recorded the date, size of the box, and time of day, 2:23 P.M., into their notebooks.

Mr. Hathaway leaned against a back wall, watching. He seldom observed my teaching and I was a little nervous with him there. I also felt it was a perfect opportunity to show him what I could do on the fly. Teachers have to be flexible. I was eager to perform.

The box was taped carefully, "This side up! Live creatures inside!" and the students giggled and squirmed as I sliced the tape and unfolded the top cautiously. I had this fleeting thought that the creatures might be loose inside, but of course, it was just several quart containers and a lot of shredded packing material. I paused. I wondered what I might find in the containers.

"Class, I hope they have arrived safely," I said. "It is difficult to send living things through the mail, though, so don't be surprised if they didn't all make it." A seriousness settled on my assembled crowd.

I reached for the first container, clearly marked CRICKETS, 40. It shuddered slightly in my hand, the tremblings of live things inside. Yuck. I felt a crawling at my neck. I carefully pried the lip of the lid open and peered inside. Eighty blinking bug eyes looked directly at me, their legs cycling at the light. I snapped it shut and swallowed hard. My stomach was queasy. I hate insects of all kinds, especially when I'm outnumbered. I put the container back in the box, my shivering hand causing a little earthquake in the paper shavings. *Get a grip,* I quickly counseled myself, *they're just crickets. They don't bite.*

"The crickets look fine," I said in this husky voice I didn't even recognize.

"Yeah!" the class cheered in unison, louder than I had expected. Several clapped and others wrote rapidly in their journals. Enthusiasm is potent stuff.

"Shhh," I warned, shifting rapidly from Wimp to Teacher. I reached for FROGS, 8. This container was larger and much heavier. I felt something move inside. I slowly forced open the lip of the container and got a quick glance at frogs upon frogs, slimy heads and dark pop eyes eager for the light. *These are big, ugly frogs,* I thought briefly as I started to close it, shrugging off a shiver of disgust.

There was a glimpse of legs extended in a flash as the top rocketed off the container and the first frog leapt to the desk of the student in front of me. The box was alive. The next moment is still in dispute; some students swear I tossed the rest to the crowd in fright, but I choose to believe the frogs simply followed their leader, popping out of the container I held stupidly outstretched before me. Frogs rained onto the heads and desks of twenty-two trusting ten-year-olds.

Screams erupted at once. Desks and chairs were overturned as students screeched and tussled, trying to escape the fleeing frogs. Students flung themselves upon each other. I stupidly held the empty container in my hand and watched my students scurry for the corners of the room. Mr. Hathaway stood dumbfounded by the back sink.

It took a minute or two for the situation to register in my head. There was no way to collect this class together. I was speechless, watching frogs leaping joyfully throughout the room. Everywhere I looked there was a frog stretching his legs, blissfully bouncing from desk to chair to floor and back again, clusters of students chasing and whooping and giggling together. I saw two boys gathered around one, hands cupped, closing in for the capture. I reached out with our container, ready to snap the top on when they had it safely incarcerated again. This moved me from stupefaction to action. I knew what to do next: catch them.

The boys closed in and the frog soared. That slimy frog face was lunging right at me, the mouth slightly open so I could see his tongue! I screamed. This shriek issued from my throat before I had thought about it. A bizarre, hysterical rhythm took over the class as each leap brought a chorus of shrieks, mine included. This continued for several minutes, I'm afraid. Mr. Hathaway was overcome by laughter, bent over at the waist, incapable of helping. I noticed several teachers peering in our door from the hall.

Somehow we gathered the eight frogs back into the quart container. After the first few it seemed to get a little easier, as the students who wanted to help did, and the rest lined up against the back wall. Before long the container was shut and back in the cardboard box. I was beginning to breathe almost naturally again. The clock said 2:43. This was enough for one day.

That thought, unfortunately, did not occur to me.

I looked around the room and considered how I could finish my lesson. I was determined to get back on track. We had set out to set up our terrariums and we would finish. Frog chase was a minor setback. On with the lesson! I might erase this disaster from memory if I got back in control and returned our minds to science. I'm an eternal optimist.

Each group gathered around, notebooks in hand, as I sprinkled a crowd of crickets into their glass observation tanks. I dispensed the two quart containers quickly and felt better knowing the bugs were out of my hands. The crickets munched on grass and crawled over their new homes and each other. My students were fascinated. Some named each one while others recorded cricket positions in their lab books. Mr. Hathaway seemed truly amazed. At least he had stopped laughing. This was a Super Teacher recovery, you have to admit.

I took a breath and reached for the frogs. They were not going to get the best of me this time. One at a time, a firm shake with one wrist while the other hand held tightly to the top. I was masterful. Not a single escape. See? I could do this.

It just hadn't occurred to me that these frogs were hungry.

Ravenous.

They had endured three long days traveling from the Midwest, the sound and smell of food so near beside them in the box. I wasn't quite prepared for cricket carnage.

The first shrieks unnerved me. I thought they signaled another escape and I whirled to see which group had foolishly let their frog out. *Not more screaming,* I thought. *Enough already; everything's under control.* Then I caught sight of what they were looking at: the frog feast. Their frog was inhaling crickets in a frenzy, cutting them in half, slurping victims off the glass as other terrified crickets clung nearby. Of course I knew the frogs were supposed to eat the crickets, but silently in the dead of the night, one lost soldier at a time. Instead, I had a horror show. Students clutched at each other, tears starting.

"Look at Petey!" Hanna moaned. Only the tail section remained.

"Cool!" several boys giggled as their frog shot across the terrarium and crickets scattered.

"Miss Ostrem! Make him stop!" I heard from across the room, turning to see a frog with at least three crickets hanging out of his mouth, the terrified legs doing a slow death dance as they advanced farther into his grinning lips.

Oh.

My.

God.

Hysteria once again took over my classroom. In those final moments, I managed to traumatize the room. The cricket population disappeared with incredible speed. In minutes the terrariums were littered with cricket parts and the few remaining insects huddled under grass or in the corners, as frogs happily surveyed their homes. There were too many tears as students grabbed coats off hooks and lined up for the buses. Girls clutched tightly to each other, refusing to hear my apologies and wishes for a good weekend. I was finished. I wanted to make this better, but I let them file out of the room and collapsed in a chair by the door. Mr. Hathaway said nothing. We listened to the roar in the hall as classrooms emptied.

Mr. Hathaway began moving chairs onto desktops and carrying terrariums back to the counter near the sink. I'm sure he couldn't imagine how he was going to comfort me, and I could feel the tears building as I watched. I managed to mumble an apology as I reached for my coat and sprang for the door. I could come in the night and collect the rest of my things, I reasoned.

It was a long weekend. I think I rewound the scene a hundred times. Each hour. By Sunday I was beginning to smile. A little. At least no one had called to fire me. I returned to school on Monday and our frogs were happily coexisting with the remaining crickets. My students chuckled about the events on Friday, but seriously recorded observations in their notebooks, and the entire unit concluded weeks later quite uneventfully.

I comforted myself, thinking that was the dumbest move I could make in teaching.

Of course I was wrong.

Not even close.

Learning doesn't follow a script; there are few perfect lessons. The unexpected might stun you one afternoon and leave you collapsing in giggles the next. Superman's cape won't protect you. In fact, I'm convinced our students don't even want flawless Super Teachers. They want human beings that unexpectedly squeal when surprised. They love it when we laugh. If our eyes fill with tears at a particularly emotional piece of student writing, it doesn't mean we've lost control. It means we're human. I now know it isn't a weakness to let that show through the façade of Teacher.

earning my stripes

It is impossible to be a teacher and a coward.

—Joan Bauer

Early one morning, my eighteen-month-old son, Cam, happily bounced above our kitchen floor singing an infant's song of chirrups and squeals to our two giant dogs splayed near him while I got ready for work. They slept, not at all interested in the hair-pulling, tail-grabbing, nose-biting toddler that was temporarily contained in a blue airplane seat, but Cam continued to serenade them. He was in a Johnny Jumper, a springy seat solidly attached by long straps to the door frame above. He could push off the floor and sway, landing gently on footed sleeper feet, knees bent, a quick kick sending him airborne again. One fist clamped in his mouth, the other draped lazily over the side, Cam was a happy, drooling boy. He loved mornings. From the moment he awoke chattering to his mobile, he began singing. It was a melody like no other, one I still hear twelve years later.

I scrambled to coordinate clean work clothes while Cam played. On this morning I had a dark blue skirt and a white shirt on, quickly flipping through my jackets for the right match. I stopped to listen. It's a mother thing: a vague sense that the background sounds have suddenly changed. I heard nothing. I called, "Cam?"

Not a sound.

I sprang to the door and quickly surmised he was still in the Johnny Jumper swing; the kidnappers, intruders, and evil fairy people receded into my dream world once more. I watched his feet kicking gently, his sounds quiet and serious. His soft cheek lay against his small fist, his eyes watching the pattern in the carpeted floor.

I crept toward him, hoping to surprise him. I whispered, "Cam," and spun him around. His arms reached out, a squeal escaping as he pressed his wet, mushy lips against my cheek. There's nothing quite like an open-mouthed baby kiss. I held him close, feeling his fists tighten around my hair. As I released him my leg felt wet and I saw a large spot of white, murky baby vomit clinging to my hose and skirt.

Damn. Another change of clothes for both of us.

I scooped Cam out of the seat and held him like a football, sprinting to his room. I was cutting it close this morning. I had always been on time, if not early; but with a baby, all had suddenly changed in my neat and ordered world. There were too many things I didn't expect each day. I didn't like my all-too-frequent speeding into the school parking lot, whipping around corners and looking for that last remaining space, always farthest from the front door. I hated rushing to my mailbox, cutting off my colleagues to whip down the hall to my classroom. I cringed if my students were in the room when I got there, sitting smugly at their seats while I peeled off my coat and tried to make small talk. It felt unprofessional.

Cam smiled while I unsnapped and resnapped, fingers working feverishly, then watched as I rushed to my closet, praying for a simple solution to my wardrobe change. Hanging before me was a white skirt: clean, coordinated, and cute. Perfect. Later, of course, I would curse this decision, rolling my eyes at my inability to think things through. But first it was in and out of the car seat, add the diaper bag, snacks, and then a quick Cam squeeze as I deposited all into Polly's arms at Day Care and dashed for the door. I made it to my seventh-grade classroom with a minute to spare.

My first group of jabbering students filled their seats and opened journals as if programmed. They listened attentively, responded appropriately, and allowed me to sail through the morning, regaining the peace I'd lost in the rush. The hum of the heater stilled me with its rhythm. I wrote of Cam, of course, my daily observations of his growth filling line after line in chunky, blue print. My students often watched me write, caught me puzzling over a word or smiling in memory, watching the moves of composition. I was their model.

My second class was the lively one. I anticipated their discussions with a mixture of amusement and fear; nothing was a sure thing. Doug sat in the front row and Jeremy three seats behind. Although recently separated, they still played off each other, and I was considering a move to the farthest corners of the room to avoid the daily wanderings off task. The problem was, sometimes I enjoyed their silliness. They were funny. Jeremy had a sharp wit and could analyze a character quickly, comparing behavior to something we could all recognize: the fry cook at KFC or the woman passing around the collection plate in church. Jeremy poked fun at all of our pretensions. Including mine.

Doug giggled and winked and made all of the girls in my class sigh. His soft, tan lashes were unbelievably long, and his voice had that deep, manly quality that seems out of character in a twelve-year-old. Doug was destined to drive a huge Ford truck. I remembered him from fourth grade, so to me he was still that funny little boy, but every girl in the class kept one eye on him at all times. He shrugged at study, hard work, and reading. He drew comics and couldn't remember his homework. He surprised me with his willingness to be Doug. He didn't need to be anyone else, a rare occurrence in middle school.

The day was warming up and I left my jacket on my chair when I rose to meet this class. I remember things started out uneventfully. I was writing something on the board when Doug's voice caught me off guard, four syllables that broke the silence.

"Nice stripes, Kittle."

My stomach lurched; I knew. I froze, crushing my chalk into the board with one hand, the other balanced on the board in front of me. I could feel my cheeks flush a furious red. I couldn't move.

The class laughed hysterically; such a frenzy of giggles I've never heard since. *Stay calm,* I pleaded. This was a first. What exactly should I do? I didn't turn around. I wanted to quickly cover my brilliantly striped blue-and-white underwear, fully visible under that perfect white skirt, but I also needed somehow to get past this moment and continue teaching. I had to ignore the fact that I had drawn attention to my underwear, my butt for Pete's sake, in front of an entire class of seventh graders! It was a thought so humiliating I thought I'd never face them again.

Teaching is truly problem solving. It's what you can't expect that can make the biggest difference on any day. I started writing the first thing that came to mind.

Doug is in BIG trouble.

My students quieted, snickering, and I bought time as I carefully formed each letter on the cold, green board before me. Could I just keep writing for the next forty minutes?

He is going to pay for this.

How? Think of something, dammit.

I had it.

"Doug, that's the most embarrassing thing that has ever happened to me in teaching," I spun around and looked directly into his eyes, ignoring the rest of the class. It was easier once I faced him; I can't say why. Maybe it's because my blue-striped butt was out of sight for the moment.

"I'm sorry, Mrs. Kittle," his eyes were sincere, but a smirk still teased at the corner of his lips.

The class studied us both. A showdown. The atmosphere was a tad tense. My classroom was frozen in time; no one dared move. I knew I ought to say something profound, since my words would undoubtedly live in each of their memories. I couldn't concentrate, however; stripes blinded my vision.

"You will have to loan me your jacket for the rest of the day so I can tie it around my waist and not embarrass myself any further." The class seemed to let out a long, steady breath.

I knew this was weak, but it was something. I wanted Doug to help with a solution, and this was as close to a natural consequence as I could muster. Doug started to protest, "I wear this everywhere," even as he uncoiled himself from the faded denim and passed it across his desk. I silently tied it around my waist, watching my students. I could feel the flush still burning in my cheeks, but the hard part was over.

"When do I get it back?" he persisted.

"Never," I replied with a cruel smile.

"Let's write," I said, curling my fingers around the spine of my journal. Pens raced along for the next ten minutes or more, the scratchings broken only by a self-conscious cough or a whimpering giggle as my mistake again came to life in their writing.

We skipped sharing our writing that day; once was enough for me.

Awkward, embarrassing moments have happened in my classroom since and I know they will happen again. We're on the spot every day, one class after another, so we're bound to draw a few laughs, to find ourselves in a room of adolescents with the word *orgasm* ("I mean *organism!*") hanging in the air. Or to bend over to retrieve something and hear a rip as fabric separates somewhere. And yes, the kids wait for those moments. We are their entertainment.

This fall I arrived at my class with a stack of books in my arms, the saga of a traveling teacher. I had been reading and noting passages I wanted to mention, color-coding my thoughts with neon Post-its. I deposited the books on a desk and began class with our morning chat and journal topic. It was at least ten minutes before Matt mentioned the yellow Post-it stuck to my right breast, an arrow pointing dead center. To crawl under my desk would be too obvious; I had to teach beyond the blush.

We all do.

one parent dies, another lives

With daily human tragedies—death of a family member, divorce, severe loneliness and depression—teachers listen and comfort, creating what is for many children the most stable space they know. In the mania for standards and test scores, this psychological work is hardly recognized.

—Tom Newkirk

Molly seemed to see the world from under her bangs, which hung in a heavy fringe over her forehead. She was a little awkward; she hung back from the others and preferred to spend time with me at recess. Molly's impish smile and quiet giggle won me over quickly. She always had something to tell me in the morning, about a bird she had seen on the way to school or how her older brother was driving her crazy again. She often greeted me with a tight hug.

Molly asked to share something with the class one day in late fall. The classroom door was still open to the playground, and we could hear the distant shouts of students filtering into their classrooms as mine hung backpacks and settled into their seats. The leaves had turned and many had fallen, so there was that damp, musty smell of the change in seasons drifting in from the long bank of windows behind my desk. Sharing was a regular part of our classroom, an informal, transitional time for students to tell about the important happenings in their lives as we all pulled on the cloak of another school day. I remember being a little annoyed when she walked to the front; it seemed to me Molly shared every day. This nine-year-old stood before the classroom, holding tightly to the chalk tray behind her, and hesitated. She didn't say a word. The class got very quiet and I looked up from my desk. Molly had her head down, both hands behind her, one heel kicking the wall.

She looked at us through tears and said, "My mother died this morning."

I can still see her standing there with a few wet spots on the front of her small T-shirt, this little child against a huge green chalkboard. I had a stack of papers in my hands, which I dropped into my lap, a breath catching in my throat. She kept one hand behind her as the other wiped away her tears. Sobs shook her.

Jon asked, "How did she die?"

I thought, *Don't ask that.* I didn't want to know. I did and I didn't. As if not explaining this could protect the rest of my class.

"She had cancer." Molly said it matter-of-factly. An evil, awful word. Almost as bad as *died.* I suddenly remembered hearing something about Molly's mom being ill; no one said dying. That seemed like an important detail someone should have shared with me. The students were silent, Molly's ragged breathing the only sound.

"Oh, Molly," I rose from my desk, "I'm so sorry." I wrapped her in my arms, her wet face buried in my sweater. The room was still; my students stunned.

I know my next thought was how to help her. I couldn't understand why she was at school. I wish I had lingered on that a bit, before trying to help. If we do our jobs right, our classrooms are families. This one certainly was, with an eclectic group of engaging, fun kids. They made me laugh every day. Over the years I've thought about the conversation that might have occurred in her house that morning, her father insisting she stay home, Molly insisting she come to school. I imagine he felt as helpless as I did. Maybe she needed to be with us.

I believe now that Molly came to class and shared because that's what our class did. We didn't just learn together; we shared our lives. I'm not sure I knew then what an impact a teacher and a classroom community can have on a child. I was new to teaching; I was a ball of energy. I was also this girl's shelter on the most awful day in her young life.

Molly stayed close to my side as I walked her down to the main office to find our guidance counselor. Molly knew Lois Williams well. Lois was a petite woman with a warm smile. In the morning Lois was usually out front by the flagpole, her black raincoat billowing behind her in the wind as she cheerfully welcomed every student by name.

Lois was in the main office talking with our secretary when we came through the door. She knelt down quickly, saying, "Molly, honey, is it Mama?"

Molly nodded, her blonde bangs bouncing, her small, chubby hands reaching out as she said, "She died, Mrs. Williams," weeping into Lois' embrace. The secretary and I looked over their heads, our eyes brimming.

I walked the long, silent path back to my classroom, breathing deeply to try to make the transition back to teacher. I was bothered by my quick resolution; I hadn't asked Molly what she wanted and I could have. I could have kept her with the class and gone in hunt of the counselor at recess. Yes, it would have been difficult and distracting and possibly not the right thing for all of my students, but I didn't even try. I passed her off.

I was relieved to find Jon and Chris out of their seats, giggling and imitating me at the chalkboard as I walked in. This was familiar territory.

In Molly's class I struggled with this very difficult student named Chris. He was ten when he came to my fourth grade, one among many, as every child is. I had a class that year of more than thirty. Chris looked a little like a chipmunk: full cheeks and large teeth. He smiled and joked constantly, a very silly boy who didn't know when to stop. Chris disrupted all of my lessons, and often more than once. He always apologized, smiling delightedly when our eyes met.

He brought little trains to school and drove them across his desk while I tried to explain the steps in multiplication. He would sharpen his pencil ten times in one lesson until I demanded he stop. He peppered me with questions, a continual assault that would leave me distracted and unable to return to what I was thinking. I was frustrated that one student was commanding so much of my attention regardless of whom I sat him next to or how I disciplined him. He spent many recess periods with me, although with his high energy, he genuinely needed the time to run around on the playground. He needed time to make friends; he didn't fit in well. I tried giving him positive reinforcement when I could. The road to June seemed impossibly long.

In frustration one afternoon, I moved his desk away from the entire class. He was back near the door, where he could play with the things in his desk without distracting others nearby. He could make comments about the lesson without forcing me to pause and address him. I found that I made it through the rest of the day with less stress than before. He stayed in that place for the rest of the week. It was easier to have Chris in the back where he could do his own thing. It wasn't the best solution, but I felt like I was regaining momentum with my class and that seemed very important.

The second week of Chris' exile, my principal stopped by for an informal visit. He spoke to Chris at the back and watched my teaching for a few minutes before moving on. He came back to see me after school. He said he was concerned about Chris' new home away from the rest of the class and asked me what my plan was for working him back into the group. I didn't have one. I was enjoying not dealing with Chris every hour. What I appreciated about this exchange was how my principal expressed confidence in me as a teacher and didn't tell me what I should do. He did, however, show how concerned he was for Chris' place with his peers and that was a powerful model. You see, it was easier to let Chris' behavior be my excuse for a new seating chart that was working for me and thirty others. I couldn't justify spending so much of my energy on one child. But that's a trap. The truth is, some students will require it. The others may be getting the attention at home that students like Chris are missing and that allows them to cope in a large class. Chris could not cope. If I ignored his lack of social skills, I wouldn't gain anything in the end, and more importantly, neither would Chris. I was going to have to find a way to reach him.

I called his house and spoke to his grandmother. She filled me in; my heart broke. He had had a long history of battles in the school, but more importantly, he was living with his grandmother because both of his parents refused to take him in. Chris' father had left years before and no one expected to see him again. Chris' mother lived in a trailer on the same property as Chris' grandparents. Mother and son were separated by perhaps two hundred yards. I don't know her story; it undoubtedly had its own horrors. What I know is that if she came to dinner, she refused to speak to Chris. His jokes did not make her laugh. If she pulled her car into the driveway and Chris was playing out front, she passed by without a wave. His grandmother told me Chris looked too much like his father, and Mom couldn't stand the sight of him. She had told him that. It hurts to even write those words down.

That story changed the way I saw Chris. He needed me. I was just as incapable as I was before I knew his story, but I was driven to help, and that is a powerful difference. I sat in meetings with specialists and we developed strategies—question cards to limit his interruptions during a lesson; smile charts for raising his hand—that I tried to make work. I was amazed that it was left to me, in my inexperience and daily mistake making, to help this child. It was some of the most challenging work I've done. At one point I had to record my directions for assignments throughout the day into a tape recorder that Chris listened to with headphones on so that he could focus. I would say, "Hey, Chris! It's Mrs. Kittle. Hope you're having a great day. Start by putting your name in the right corner of your paper . . . ," and I would see Chris sitting at the back with the headphones on, smiling at me. But I also saw that little boy sitting away from the class with his own educational plan while the rest of us went on with a lesson, and I knew this wasn't the right solution.

This was well before the Ritalin rush. Chris wasn't diagnosed with ADHD, although he surely had more of the symptoms than many of my students who've been diagnosed with it in the last few years. I believe medication might have made a difference for him, but no one pursued it. I tried every management trick you can imagine. I'd like to say my attempts were successful, but in the end, I'm not sure. I know he had a mostly positive year in my class and participated in cooperative groups to complete work. He found a place *in* my class, not at the back of it.

Although I may not have such dramatic events in my room this year, I should certainly expect the child who buried the family pet the night before or learned of a grandparent's serious illness. These are earthquakes in the lives of my students. I should expect that some will witness battles between their parents and fear divorce, some will be treated rudely by a best friend and feel unable to think straight. Daily life intrudes. We cannot ignore it and just keep teaching the causes of the Civil War.

You have to wonder: what exactly are we accountable for? Imagine if I had written the whole truth on their report cards.

> *Chris struggled to understand his mother's rejection while mastering multiplication of two-digit numbers. He walked by her house each morning on his way to the bus, and if she saw him, she ignored him, but he could name all of the states and their capitals.*
>
> *Molly buried her mother this school year. She may have longed for her during the afternoon, but she could link all of her letters in cursive and answer the comprehension questions correctly.*

I have learned to watch and listen for the secret lives of my students. It's what I don't see at first that can make all the difference.

below average

When I look back at my education, which I avoid doing, and my children's education, I am stunned by the amount of dull, dumb, superficial waste-of-time work.

—Donald Murray

I was a natural artist. It was one of my few escapes from a household sighing under the weight of alcoholism. I thought my father drank because I ran too loudly through the house or fought cruelly with my older sister. Better to be silent, I reasoned. I found shelter in art and in books. I was better at drawing than most other things, and I harbored a secret fondness for it that was very precious indeed.

My art teacher was a small, spindly woman with a serious, plain look. She could not smile. I'm sure of that. The muscles had simply forgotten how to relax. She had eyes that watched everything. There was no kindness there. I was put at a back table against the wall and ignored for our weekly lessons. As a child believes in a teacher's intuitive power and carefully mastered instinct, I believed she put me there because it was my place. I belonged against the wall, out of sight, lest I might corrupt others. After all, it was my assigned seat. Assigned by God, I imagined.

At some point in the year I found myself miraculously at one of the center tables in the classroom. I am convinced today it was because of my work. In a room of children, I had something and she wanted me nearer. She had never told me my work was good; I only knew because she said so little to me at all. She found less to correct in my drawings than in my classmates'. Her classroom was composed of corrections, but never praise. I did not expect encouragement there.

The assignment was to draw the student perched on a chair high above us on a table without taking our eyes off of him. She was clear in her directions. Our pencils were not to leave the pages, our eyes not to leave the subject. I was stymied; how does one draw without seeing? I had learned to see by studying light, shadow, and form. I knew the curve of a shoulder, the sharpness of an elbow, the almost flat surface of the table that stretched before me. To draw I had to make my page become the thing before me. I knew how to do that and I could be lost for hours in the slats of a chair or the curve of a tennis ball can. It is a wonderful thing for a child to find a passion like this and have success. Particularly a child that has a home filled with shadows and confusion. I didn't dream of being an artist, however. I didn't dream of much at all. At twelve, I simply walked through my days trying to make as small an imprint as possible. From somewhere deep inside I treasured this simple talent, though. It was mine.

Today David sat primly in the seat before me and the rest of the class, happily freed from drawing. He was a perfect model, motionless, willing to do this well. I couldn't begin. I saw the folds in his shirt and the way the sunlight dusted across the top of his head, one hair rising in a crooked path toward the ceiling. My eyes traced his profile to the fullness in his lips, so smooth they made me blush and I instinctively lowered my gaze. There was nothing on the page before me. I looked up again and willed my pencil to move. A line began—the edge of his shirt, along his forearm to the elbow. I resisted the urge to look down. There must be something to this—she's the teacher after all. I could do it. I would concentrate and keep drawing.

Our teacher paced the space between us, barking often, "You may not look!" or "Faster!" a few students giggling as their pencils skated across paper. "Keep drawing! Fill the page!" I continued one, thin line across his lap and could feel the turn for the knee. My pencil abruptly left the page and marked the table. I jolted to wipe away the mark and even before I had formed the thought, glanced at my work. It was meaningless. A long, thin line that left no impression whatsoever. My heart was thumping wildly. I could feel a tremor in my hand. The loops of pencils continued all around me and my stomach turned. I hastily returned my pencil to center and started again. I tried to move faster. I could see a few drawings near me and they were a mess—a child's scribbles. I tried to imitate that. I gave up precision for large lines and big strokes. I simply couldn't do it blind; I had to sneak a look to do any work at all. I only looked when the teacher was away and I didn't look *all* of the time. I began to enjoy how far from real my drawing was, certainly one of my worst.

"Time's up," her voice called, "sign your work and line up for grading!" She moved sprightly to her desk and seized a red pen from the tray before her. Class always ended this way. We made a line at her desk and she graded each piece, then we made a line at the door. We chatted in line, comparing our work, laughing.

"Mine's an F," Kirk beamed. He usually hid his drawing against his chest or pretended it away with loud talk in line. Today he was pleased. His looked like all the others.

"Penny's is good. Wow. Yours almost looks like a person. You'll get an A for sure," Susan nodded as Cynthia praised my work. I needed to hear this. I always needed to hear it.

We inched closer to her desk.

Many students had As, an unusual day. There were squeals of delight. The boys jostled each other and held their red As up for the girls to see. I didn't understand. None of them looked like David. Or a chair. Or anything at all. Yet with just a glance, our teacher wrote A at the corner time and time again. I watched students passing by me and felt increasingly sure I would receive an A, possibly an A+. Mine was by far the best.

"How did you do that?" Julia asked, staring carefully at my work. "Did you cheat?"

I froze.

"You did, didn't you?" she whispered fiercely in my ear. To anyone else a lie would have been spit quickly into the space between us. *Of course I didn't cheat.* But this was Julia, my best friend. I hesitated. "Don't worry, I won't tell," she offered quietly.

She was next. Julia's paper was a wild series of wavy lines. She sighed and slowly passed her paper to the teacher. She stepped on one foot with her other and lowered her head so that I could see the small hairs at the back of her neck below her thick ponytail.

"Excellent, Julia," the teacher replied crisply, her pen scratching a glorious A on the right corner. Julia grinned at me, grabbed her drawing, and moved to the long line of students waiting at the classroom door for the last few of us to finish. From the open windows above them I could hear the laughter on the playground. Faraway voices played chase and hopscotch and kickball. Recess would come soon after we returned to our classroom from art. I stood listening, imagining joining them when Ms. Haley's sharp voice roused me.

"Penny!"

The class giggled as I jumped and quickly put my drawing before her. I was sure I heard it: a quick intake of breath when she looked at my work. She said nothing. The room seemed to pause around me, waiting. Her silence got the attention of the class. No one moved.

With a short sigh she reached for her red pen and said loudly, "You looked."

She said it matter-of-factly.

Seriously.

No question about it.

Guilty.

I could feel my face reddening, the heat pulsing off my cheeks and the tears coming quickly to my eyes. Ms. Haley seemed to enjoy her next move. She wrote a large C- at the bottom of my work. She didn't look at me as she passed it to me; I could feel how my work disgusted her. I wished it would disintegrate in my hands so I might delete this moment from my life. A giant pink eraser could wipe my image from this place and I would never return.

I remember a slow walk home that day. The hill that climbed to our house was shady with the branches of many old trees. As cars passed I turned my head from the road. I held my crumpled drawing in my right fist. I kept seeing the C-. I had memorized the path her pen had taken to grade my work. It was an ugly, angry letter. I had never had one like it. Never. In fact, I was sure no one in my family had ever had a C. My sister was a straight-A student in high school already and my mom sat tall when she said, "She's following my path; I had all As in high school and was the valedictorian." I could feel her disappointment in me before she'd even seen my work.

But of course this made sense; I deserved this letter. I would never be my sister or my mother. I was the Other at our house. "The only blonde in four generations," my father was quick to remind me. He said this with amusement and pleasure in his eyes, and he softened when he reached out to put his hand on my head. My sister, however, said my blonde hair was a sure sign of my adoption.

"You don't belong in this family you know," she said confidently, "you were adopted when I was five. Your parents didn't want you." Older sisters know things, so I believed her. I didn't have the heart to ask my mother if it was true. In fact, I don't believe I mentioned it for another ten years.

I destroyed my drawing, of course. My family never knew. I dreaded my grades that quarter, expecting the C- to appear on my report card as further punishment. I answered every phone call that came in, but Ms. Haley never called. They never knew because I received the usual A that quarter, a deep mystery to me.

I learned two things that year with Ms. Haley. Watch out for teachers; their surprises can be wicked. When you think you understand what they're up to, you could be wrong. Terribly wrong. And I learned to disappear to the back of a classroom—never a problem, never a participant. I learned the power of being invisible. I lost something important that year as well. I lost the joy I had known in art. I was afraid to try, afraid to be wrong. I didn't draw for years. Teachers have great power, and thus, great responsibility.

The seeds from that day in Ms. Haley's room grew, for that was the year I decided to become a teacher. Perhaps many go into teaching simply to right a wrong from the past.

one kid at a time

Having children depend on you makes you strong.
Because listening to them makes you wiser.

—Judy Blume

lair is the boy who rarely does his homework, the boy who never raises his hand. He has brown curly hair that creeps out from under his hat. He has glasses and a wide smile, but rarely speaks first. There's always at least one of these in a class, it seems. He answers politely if I call on him, but days can go by and we won't speak: he, lost in a class of twenty-nine, me, rushing to keep things hopping. I ask for work, remind him of missing assignments, but see only the bare minimum from him. Every time. It's easy to think that's all he's capable of, but that never satisfies me. That word *can't* just sticks in my throat. *Won't* is more like it, and why exactly? That's the real question.

When I ask, Blair says he's never liked English. He doesn't like reading. He seems eager not to hurt my feelings, "I really like your class, Mrs. Kittle." Blair has these large, blue eyes that are filled with kindness. You know he puts food out for stray cats or stops to pick up something an older woman drops in his path.

Today Blair was out enjoying the falling snow as class assembled. We had all hoped for a snow day, or at least a late opening, but school started on time and we reluctantly came in from the first real buildup of the year. Blair has a handful of snow, ready to throw at Steve, who nailed him on the cheek just seconds before I opened my door. He's disappointed

I've stopped him, but he respects my authority and complies. He takes a bite, then scoots in, half a snowball in the palm of his red hand.

"No snow in my classroom," it's so obvious I can't believe I have to say it.

"I'm just going to eat it," he says as he takes a small bite and smiles. I almost believe him, and that hesitation costs me.

Keith, who is coming up behind him, smacks Blair's hand to dislodge it and Blair responds with a perfect baseball pitch that scatters white stuff into Keith's ear and across his face. It misses me by inches. That fast. A second or two and I've got snowballs whizzing in my room. This is the stuff they don't explain in teacher education.

"Lunch with me, Blair," it's that serious teacher tone I save for occasions like this.

The class roars. You remember high school: lunch is critical social time. I turn to pick up my grade book and see Josh send one up to the front row. He can't believe I saw him at the last minute. He flashes me a big smile.

"You too, Josh." I'm starting to get angry. I'm hovering on the edge of class mutiny; I can feel it.

"This feels like junior high. Lunch detention!" Josh whines.

"Okay, after school. I'm going to be here anyway," not even a trace of a smile now and my voice has a decided edge to it.

"Lunch is fine," he sulks into his chair.

Blair shows up with pizza and four bags of chips, on time. He sits at the table and we chat about skiing. The winter weather swirls at my window. I taunted him recently with snow reports from Oregon, our destination for the Christmas break. There are fourteen feet of snow on Mount Hood already. Blair's envy is genuine. He's never skied in powder to his knees. He's never been on an airplane.

Lunch detention is just one more opportunity to get to know my students, so I drop what I'm doing and listen. Blair tells me he placed eighth in a ski race two years ago and ended up at the Junior

Olympics. His next year he was in the top twenty in the country, then he took a bad fall and twisted up his knee. He hasn't lost his speed, but all the other kids were improving while he was convalescing, so he can't regain his standing.

His pizza is congealing, but he's still talking.

His grandfather was a great skier; they named a local award after him. Blair is proud of him. He says he wanted to earn that award himself before he left elementary school, and finally accomplished it in sixth grade. He beams.

There is so much I didn't know about this kid. So much that will make my teaching better. Think about it: he was hurt just as his ski career started to rise. He can connect to the characters we've read that are blindsided and struggle on. If I knew as much about every student as I now know about Blair, I could help them see themselves in the stories we read. I can use that to hook them and get them reading.

I see myself booking lunch with every one of my students in this class. Twenty-nine straight days. And that's for just one class! It would take six weeks. I can't give up lunch for six weeks; the twenty minutes I'd lose each day would hurt. Teachers use every minute. Then think of the students who would forget, intentionally or not. I've got to track them down because if I don't, they'll assume I don't really care. Some will need to be asked more than once. Some conversations will be awkward. Let's face it: for some, having lunch with me *would* be a punishment. Some would be absent when their day came and I'd get a whole lot of other things done during that time. That would temper my enthusiasm. It is why I don't show up at class the next day with my calendar in hand. I silently vow next term to start that way, before things get hectic.

It always feels possible.

It isn't.

I will try to reach every student, but in the end it is a bit like Karma to me—I connect well to some that cross my path, and try not to fret about all of those I miss. I regret that the conditions of school have forced this concession on me, but I accept it. I can hope to make a difference with some, not all. It is why I teach here in the White Mountains; we have reasonable class sizes. When you give teachers two hundred students a day in an inner city filled with heartbreak, you guarantee compromises that hurt kids. What a difference we could make if we capped classes at twenty all over this country and allowed all teachers time to develop meaningful relationships with students.

Blair finishes cold pizza. Our time is up. He says, "This was my punishment?"

I say almost completely seriously, "Yes. Your time and this lecture: You know you can't bring snow, throw snow, eat snow, or *think* snow while you're in my class, right?"

"Yes," small grin.

"Then we're done."

"Thanks, Mrs. Kittle."

beneath white icing

A well-spun tale will calm even the warrior. Stories help us make sense
of the universe. They mend the pieces of a broken spirit.

—Laurie Halse Anderson

I passed out playing cards to each student as they arrived in class one morning, hoping that a gimmick might nudge my determined rebels into writing. I asked them to look at the number and remember a story from that year in their life. They could trade cards if they wanted, but I encouraged them to try to work with the number they had. Conversations began as I finished attendance. Writing is always easier if students begin by telling the stories first; it is a natural medium for them.

Jesse shared his pursuit of girls on the playground in third grade and we all laughed. Donald mentioned going on a long-distance trip with his father, a truck driver. I had chills. I knew from his journal that his father had died when he was eight, and that this was a precious, important story. Derek had a jack of hearts, and he spoke of his first time getting drunk.

Jenny asked, "What number is a jack?"

"Eleven," he answered.

This spawned too many stories of drunkenness, parties, and reckless driving stunts. My juniors and seniors were eager to outdo one another. The tempo shifted when I called on Heather. She began talking about a move across several states. Most of my students had been uprooted before. One girl was on her thirteenth move. The stories quickly changed to ones of loss and need. We kept track of categories of memories on the chalkboard: firsts, birthdays, celebrations, moves, and so on. I asked them to pick one of the stories they remembered and write for fifteen minutes.

It is beautiful to watch pens marching in unison across blank pages. I hate to call "time" when many are writing. Linda Rief spoke about this at a conference I attended. She said we shouldn't be afraid to stop writing because if you stop mid-sentence, it is easier to come back to where you left off the next day. I still can't end in the middle of a thought, but I have found it is easy to come back if I stop mid-story. I know it will be for my students as well. It is better to leave them wishing they had time to write more than tapping their pencils in boredom as others finish.

It was early in our work together and only one student was willing to share his writing when drafting ended that day. I collected the rest and read eagerly that evening. It was a somewhat typical collection of adolescent stories, except for one. Steven wrote rage. His words were vile and centered on one cocky boy who sat midway back in the row beside him. I knew these two were enemies and had asked Steven to move away from Jason earlier in the week because their whispered hostilities kept interrupting our work. Steven was an outcast. I can never figure out exactly how it begins with some children, but it is a cancer that continues to destroy once it starts. Steven had been a target for years and had worked hard to develop a complicated defense strategy. He always went out the opposite door as Jason and his friends at the end of class. He told me during the first week of school that he liked to sit where he could keep the entire class in view at all times. He wrote in his journal of controlling his own anger and of his faith in God.

Steven's draft was shocking. It was as bad as the most profane rap I've heard with vivid images of violence, hatred, and destruction. I confess the class had asked before we started if they could swear in their drafts, and I had told them it was just drafting, so it was okay. I knew it was a risk. Only a few students used any profanity, but there was a sense of freedom and openness that settled on the class when I gave them an invitation to tell the truth, however it came out. This piece was truly horrible, far worse than I had expected from any of my students. I brought it home and said to my husband, "Listen to what this kid wrote."

Pat knew I was struggling with this collection of unmotivated readers and writers. He raised one eyebrow as I read the words aloud. A mixture of amusement and disdain surfaced on his face. When I finished, he said curtly, "Is that acceptable?" It was the sound of Pat Robertson and all the conservative critics of our work. It was the sound of people who don't understand at all what it means to teach.

"Of course it isn't," I sizzled. "Of course this isn't what I wanted Steven to write." I could feel my teeth clench.

"What are you going to do about it?" he challenged me.

I resented this test. My husband has always been a great sounding board about my life in teaching. Each year he knows my students by name. He helps me think through solutions and listens patiently to the roller coaster of emotions I bring home each week. But at times he just doesn't get it, just as I will never fully understand his management of paper mills. What he does get is when to back off. He can see it in my eyes. He was sympathetic when I answered, "I don't know exactly," and we moved on to steaming broccoli and setting the table.

The next day I handed back drafts to students as we prepared to write again. I told them they could continue the story they had started, or begin another. I handed Steven his, saying, "Is this what you want to write about?"

He answered quickly, "No, I have another story in mind." He removed his hood. He had a handsome face and an engaging smile that was too often hidden behind a black sweatshirt pulled tight against his filthy baseball hat. I wondered if removing the hood was a signal that I had passed his test by not passing judgment on what he had needed to say. He wrote freely, more slowly, that day, but many did not. Writing did not come easily for this class. In the first burst of writing they had stories to tell. Without the buildup of playing cards and brainstormed lists, this second day of drafting was work for most. These kids didn't like to be frustrated; they wouldn't try for long. There were spitballs and whispers. Fifteen minutes shrank to eight.

I decided on a new jumping-off place for the next day, which happened to be Valentine's Day. The sense of smell is a powerful key to our memories. I baked vanilla cupcakes that night and covered them with fluffy, white frosting and red sugar sprinkles. I wrote out a tiny Valentine card for each student. When I brought them to class I told the students I was giving them two links to their past. I made them smell the frosting and think before they ripped off the wrappers and inhaled the cupcakes. We briefly talked about other frosting-related memories, making another brainstorm list for our chalkboard. Backyard birthday parties, cake fights, surprise creations for Mother's Day, and grandma's kitchen made the list. Memories flooded the pages they held and everyone found something to say, writing beyond our fifteen-minute goal. Three students shared their writing. Steven did not. This is what I found when I began reading that night at home:

I really can't say the sight/smell of the cupcake caused any feelings in me besides hunger. Valentine's Day was never my favorite holiday, the only thing I liked about it was the candy and parties during class time. I have no romantic memories of this time of year. In truth it is one of my least favorite holidays. In elementary school I was given Valentines only because it was required for everyone to get them. I was always last on everyone's minds for Valentine's Day. I remember children of my class, fueled by youth and freedom, passing out crimson hearts and colorful cards to each other with smiles, but the smiles faded when it came to me. I, of course, passed them out as well, but sooner or later they found their way to the trash. During the parties people formed groups, like prides of lions, to laugh and have fun, but I was always the outcast, the one certainly not invited to join them. And so for that reason I am not a fan of Valentine's Day. Cupid's arrows bounce off as if I'm wearing armor now. The warm passion has gone cold.

Beneath Steven's rage is a searing pain that has been silenced for years. His writing is clear; his voice strong. He has images in that short first draft that are vivid and show a writer ready to bloom. I can build on that. I can show him how to structure his writing to lead his readers along. I can teach him conventions that focus thought. If Steven knows what he wants to say, I can help him say it well.

I believe Steven had to speak the rage first, to get to the vulnerability he'd rather not face. It may be that next year Steven will go to his English class and write something as profane as that first piece I read of his. He might be disciplined and defend himself with my acceptance of such raw writing. I may be chastised by colleagues and misunderstood by my principal, but I just couldn't discipline a child for writing his truth. Adolescents are sometimes sensitive, bleeding, and crude. If we get beneath that, we might find a voice that speaks of fear and uncertainty, on the brink of discovery. We can move the writer and the child forward by searching for stories that surface after the wrath.

haunted

Rivers of rage run from one generation to another,
and it may be impossible to staunch the flow.
—*Christopher Scanlan*

I left college eager to reach every child, and sure somehow I would find a way. It is more difficult than I imagined; in fact, I fail at it with some kids every year. I've found myself chasing after these students in my sleep for years after they have left my classroom, trying to see what I could have done differently. This reflection is powerful fuel. I know there are students I couldn't reach ten years ago that I could find a path to today. It will always be that way. I will always learn from my students at least as much as they learn from me.

I think that is part of what saddens me over the loss of so many young teachers in our schools. They flee before they have a chance to watch themselves improve over time and realize the dreams they began teaching with. It isn't that the job gets easier, because it does only slightly, as you gain experience; it is that you get more efficient, proficient, and wise.

I want to tell you a story of three students I didn't help. I'm not taking the blame for their failures, but I'm willing to take the blame for my own. All of these students have now dropped out of school. I will probably never see them again.

Billy

Billy Brown arrived in my advisory group, unannounced, mid-fall. He was taken in by relatives in our quiet town, in hopes of changing his life course. He was repeating eighth grade. In his previous hometown he had spent almost the entire school year wandering the streets with a gang of hoodlums, his mother lost to a drug habit. His father had been absent for years. Billy had decided to steal his way into adulthood, and the kindness of his aunt and uncle was a last resort. Either Billy would make it here in the mountains, or he would return and serve out his sentence.

I liked Billy. He had a husky voice and an easy laugh. He blushed when I baked a cake for his birthday and we sang to him. I could imagine this transplant across the United States wasn't his first choice. He arrived in our town with two tiny movie theatres and not a friend in sight. That's a tough road at fifteen. He had messy, brown hair and small, blue eyes. The toughest girls liked him a lot. The others enjoyed his bravado, his carefree "I'm not doing it" stance toward school and his stories of life in another world. Of course, those are the parts that I didn't like at all. I'd suggest a book and he'd roll his eyes. When you think about it, even *The Outsiders* is kind of a joke if you've lived a life like his. The books that are tougher than that, that might connect to him and get him reading, would never make it past my school board. Billy's life was a four-letter word.

This boy was barely literate. He struggled to comprehend one page while my other students raced along, devouring whole books in a weekend. The testing and paperwork for special education takes months to complete, so I knew I was it. It is hard to accommodate this level of need in a regular classroom. Some days I didn't try very hard; I turned to other students more willing to work with me.

We had a writing workshop in my classroom and students were allowed to choose their own topics. Billy arrived during a personal narrative unit. I was teaching students the tools storytellers use and asking them to pursue pieces from their childhood. Students shared drafts daily in author's chair and worked together often during class time. Billy seemed to enjoy the activity, but he wasn't participating. His journal entries consisted of "Hey, Mrs. Kittle, how ya doing?" Maybe a sentence or two on his youngest cousin, but nothing he would build on. I encouraged him to work on one of my classroom computers, since his handwriting was horrid and he'd had almost no experience with technology. He loved writing, highlighting, deleting. I'd look across the room and see him plunking along, ten sentences or more on the screen, then flash, it was gone. I asked him to save his work; he refused. The one time I got behind him and read what he had written, I gasped. He enjoyed that. It was a story of stealing an old woman's purse, a hunter stalking his prey, sizing up his kill. His voice stunned me. He had enjoyed the old woman's fear, and I trembled as I read.

Billy was absent at least once a week. Sometimes many days at a time. Our team met with his aunt and uncle and listened to the horrors of adding him to their household. It was straining their marriage and complicating their parenting of younger children. We were frustrated, they even more so. He returned from absences to disrupt our classes, settled in for a day or two, then was absent again. He was accumulating a fierce group of friends that met him after school and did things that made us cringe.

I wanted to civilize him.

Abruptly one Friday he was gone. The students told me he had been put on a plane back to his mother's that morning. The counselor confirmed it. He hadn't been told it was happening; there were no tearful good-byes. The aunt and uncle had decided to save their own family and let him go. The counselor told us he returned to juvenile court, and eventually to jail. My students briefly mourned his absence, sure he would be back by June, but seemed to forget him before the snow was gone.

It's easy to say he was lost before he got to me; it wasn't my fault. But I also failed him. Billy's story of the robbery was his story to tell.

I didn't like it. I didn't treat it like a draft; I treated it like a sin. I could have allowed the robbery to be an invitation into working with him on his writing. He needed my acceptance; I wanted his stories to be different. I didn't encourage him to share his story in author's chair because I didn't want to celebrate what he had done. I didn't want him to tell the truth in his writing, something I preached regularly in mini-lessons. He surely saw that contradiction. You see, when we give our students the keys to writing topics they care about, we have to go all the way. We can't stop and say, "No, not that one, write about this one." Some of our students have brutal stories to tell. If I have the courage to let them pursue those topics, the stories will teach. Perhaps Billy wanted to write that story to confront his own nagging belief that what he'd done was wrong. I confess I asked him to write about something else that day in my room. I missed my chance with him, the only one I had.

This is what keeps me from despair: Billy is sitting at a table with a book before him. He got it out of the prison library because there wasn't anything else to do and he remembered Mrs. Kittle had said it was worth reading. He meets real people on the pages, stories he can feel and understand. He thinks about what he's reading. He begins to see. And that makes all the difference.

It could happen.

Peter

Peter was a tough guy, but he didn't look it at first glance. Peter's eyes smiled: beautiful, doelike, hazy blue, and sparkling with intelligence and wit. Peter's smile was perfect: straight, white teeth. He had a Pillsbury Doughboy kind of body, seemingly soft and pliable, but what came out of his mouth was pure acid; he intended to harm.

Peter scared most of the students on our team and they kept their distance. He gathered a few boys around him at lunch and leered at the girls, his whispered comments a combustible mix of anger and lust. There was no question of his intent. I fought the dichotomy in my own mind, to protect my other students, to understand the insecurity that Peter wore with his oversized jeans. I don't remember Peter's writing; I remember judging his body language each afternoon to determine what kind of a day we were going to have. I watched him watch others, anticipating arguments, challenges, fistfights. This was lion taming, not teaching.

Peter stunned me when I introduced him to Shakespeare. He read it more naturally than I did. His first attempt with *Romeo and Juliet* was fluent and melodic. Peter found the rhythm in the poetry without studying it. He pronounced a myriad of unfamiliar words with ease; he gave Romeo life and passion. He didn't just speak it, he understood the imagery. Peter was excellent in those days; I just didn't know how to keep him there.

That same week he told his math teacher to "suck his dick" and then retold this story to my class. I sent him into the hall, so I could speak to him privately. He punched in a locker near my door, deep, ferocious dents that remain today. I was told by his father that Peter couldn't control his swearing; it was his language. He spoke that way at home. I said that was a problem. The previous day he had raged at our counselor in the hall, calling her names I won't repeat. I told Peter and his father that the language wouldn't be tolerated in my classroom. It was a small line in the sand, but I drew it purposefully. It was too much to ask of me.

Profanity is a challenge. I have told students to delete it and mask it with symbols and write around it. But they speak it. They sing it. They listen to it in movies, on television, and in their homes. This is part of their language. I can refuse to hear it in my classroom, but do I lose my chance with those students as well?

I saw Peter when I went to observe one of my new teachers this fall. He smiled, made small talk, and let me sit next to him. He told me he was two weeks from his birthday, the magic sixteen, when he was going to walk out of school without a look back. He couldn't wait. I asked him what he planned to do.

Nothing.

He's still doing it, waiting at a convenience store for friends to leave the building some days after school, smoking cigarettes, watching traffic. I heard he pumps gas somewhere along the highway. There isn't a lot of beauty in a life that's hostile.

He was too much for me. I was in the way, another orange traffic cone to maneuver around on his way to dropping out. And for all my college coursework, for all my hours of thought devoted to at-risk adolescents, I couldn't change his course, although I'm expected to. If he wrote what he was thinking on a standardized test, his failure would be called mine. That's the current language about education in America: teachers should be held accountable. Teachers and schools are failing our students. Perhaps if I'd tried something else Peter would still be in school. I'll never know.

I hope Peter finds his way back to Shakespeare. I hope he remembers those moments gathered around the back table by my window, with the spring sunlight warming our backs, and Romeo's pursuit of Tybalt gripping our hearts.

> A glooming peace this morning with it brings;
> The sun for sorrow will not show his head.
> Go hence, to have more talk of these sad things. . . .

Andrea

Andrea was another transplant. From Los Angeles to Conway, from the city to a small town, from her family to an aunt she hardly knew. Andrea's mother was put in jail and this was the only place for Andrea to go. She was furious. She arrived on Christmas Eve and it was snowing.

The first time I remember really seeing Andrea was at our hospital, this beautiful white building that sits on a hill, a flood of windows across the front. Andrea was in a room down a long hall. She had tried to kill herself the night before. She sat in her room at the edge of her bed in fluffy slippers and flannel pajamas. This girl was just so alone.

Andrea had chocolate brown eyes and long, dark hair with a slight wave. She smiled when I walked in and reached for the rose I held, inhaling its scent with a dreamy look. It was awkward. I asked how she was and she said, "Better." Her aunt arrived and I made my exit, telling her I looked forward to seeing her at school.

Andrea returned the following week. She loved journal writing; she also loved talking. She had a temper. She yelled in the halls. She frightened some of the girls and all of the boys. Andrea knew things. She wore her clothes tight and tossed her hair back as she pushed out her chest, sizing up the high school boys she went out of her way to find in the halls and parking lots. She had a quick series of boyfriends.

Suddenly Andrea moved to foster care; something had gone very wrong at her aunt's house. This was a dangerous time. It was a group home and the others there didn't seem likely to help Andrea. She spoke of running away, trying to find her way back to California. I remember a fleeting thought of taking her in myself, although I had learned long ago to let that go. Too many children have come along that I've wanted to parent. Andrea wasn't any different. There was a real sweetness in her that I wanted to nurture; there was a hardness there I couldn't quite understand.

Andrea quickly became very attached to her foster mother, Darlene. She wrote of her every day in her journal. She called her Mom. We were starting our December writing project and I encouraged her to focus it on Darlene. My students were asked to make a fabric book and fill it with their writing, a present for someone they cared about. I had parents come to class and help create the books; it was a festive, fun atmosphere. Andrea crafted her book carefully, hand sewing the pages and using stencils to make her letters perfect. With piano music playing, my students worked diligently in quiet conversation to create their presents. Andrea worked right beside them.

Our battles had ended. Andrea had her materials out when class started. She was quiet and composed throughout the hour and rarely swore or stared menacingly at anyone. She didn't tell me the work was stupid; she didn't sneer when the classical music started. She seemed peaceful, almost happy, her hair spilling all over her desk, a handful of colored pencils beside her as she worked. She stopped talking about running away.

It didn't last long. When the project ended, Andrea refused to do anything else. She came late to my "worthless" class because she had to. She glared at me if I shushed her while I was teaching. She tore up all of the drafts in her writing folder and ceremoniously deposited them in the trash can one day as my other students looked nervously on. Andrea would not read. I tried to be pleasant; I confess I was often impatient, frustrated, and intolerant. I was trying to fix everything too quickly with her, sure I was going to run out of time. She didn't share my sense of urgency.

And just like that, she was gone.

She stole money from Darlene and left town with three others.

The police tried tracking them.

Not a trace.

My hope for Andrea is that by giving her poems and so much of herself in that hand-sewn Christmas book, she felt the healing power of giving. I also hope that poetry will provide strength for her journey.

My problem is, I really do want to save them all; I can't believe anyone is a lost cause. And then when I lose a few, I don't want to play this game anymore. I contemplate applying to private schools that can just toss students this tough. I mull over returning to college teaching, where students are eager to listen. I consider packing up my books and leaving public schools for good. I'd miss watching kids devour Shakespeare, but I'd stop lying awake at two A.M. worrying about Peter and the rest of those I can't reach.

I've learned instead to embrace the haunting. My former failures help the students who have walked into my room this year. I try to change what didn't work with my toughest cases, and use those lessons to succeed with others.

It works, but it is a poignant victory.

donuts to dollars

"It is our choices, Harry, that show what we truly are,
far more than our abilities."
Professor Dumbledore to Harry in
Harry Potter and the Chamber of Secrets

—J. K. Rowling

Mike completed every assignment. He wrote confidently, was rarely absent, and consumed Harry Potter books. For his third time. He was serious and mature, clearly focused on not only finishing high school, but going out strong. Mike's eyes smiled; he was easy to talk to. He sped through our class novels so he could get back to Harry. He folded his hands before him on the desk and leaned over the pages reverently, a smile just at the corner of his mouth as his eyes darted line to line. I liked that he read something so playful, and wasn't embarrassed to haul it out of his backpack each day. Mike didn't need to strut and swagger like so many other young men in my class.

One time I had a substitute that came late. Fifteen minutes late. A dozen students decided they didn't need to wait for anyone and took off. When I saw the list the next day, I sighed at all of the names, but Mike's surprised me. I asked him what he had done with the time. He said he had taken *The Goblet of Fire* and gone to sit under the bleachers in the field to read. I could imagine him reclined on the grass, his feet up on a metal rung, the wind fluttering across the pages as he studied them. He knew the substitute would just waste his time and he wasn't putting up with it, he said. He was two-hundred pages farther than he had been the day before, but of course, he was disciplined by the vice principal. I liked the thought of him finding a place to read; I really can't say he did less than those that remained in class.

At the start of fourth quarter in April, pre-spring, my class started sensing a release from school for the summer. It comes earlier every year. Their feet drum the floor, they write half as much as they did in winter, and they beg to go outside. I wanted writing to give them freedom, while also refocusing our efforts for the end of the year. I told them we were going to attempt a series of snapshots about learning, then weave them together to reflect on the moments that had made them successful learners, and those that had frustrated them and set them back. I was teaching organization and transitions in writing, but also hoping this group of disaffected students would uncover the real reasons they often refused to work in school. I hoped they would acknowledge previous work that had been meaningful and lasting, but truthfully, I expected a lot of whining. I was wrong.

I began with a few I had written, then used a series of prompts, poetry, and student models to encourage quick writes each day in class. I was stunned at all they had to say. Students wrote painfully about failing in elementary school and battling with their parents and teachers. Most wrote about early involvement with drugs and alcohol, the twin omens of ruin. My class took this writing seriously; they had stories to tell. And they were willing to share. Each day students hesitantly read their short pieces, exposing their lives for class consumption. It was gutsy work and it drew us together. We laughed at moments from elementary school, then sat in complete silence when Brittany spoke of losing her younger sister and being unable to concentrate in school for years after.

Mike wrote about raging at authority, bringing a knife to school, and feeling lost in the storm of adolescence. He reflected on his success in our alternative education program, how it had saved him when he was expelled and then taught him how to learn. Mike's final draft ended with,

I've made it. I am graduating in June and I've already been accepted to technical college. I have survived.

I thanked him for letting me know it was possible. Mike's story showed me that from the lowest point, a student can still rise and conquer.

On a Friday morning in May I glanced at our local paper before class. "North Conway Man and a Juvenile Arrested for Dunkin' Donuts Robbery." I began reading with some interest. Our town is small; crime is rare. In the first paragraph the man was identified as my student Mike. I kept rereading his name, thinking, *He's not a man, he's a kid.* And I tried to ignore the panic I felt. This would change everything.

Mike was absent. I thought about him over the weekend, wondering how someone so close could fall so far, and if there was anything I could do to help. Criminal or not, this was a kid I cared very much about.

On Monday he was back. My class immediately wanted to know what was happening with him. Two other students had been arrested over the weekend for possession of a controlled substance. I didn't like the trend. We shouldn't be able to compare experiences with handcuffs and police cars; school should be about literature and science, but our classrooms teem with life. My lesson wasn't moving forward until we had heard from Mike.

"Dude, what happened?" Brian asked.

"Well, the paper got everything wrong," Mike shot the words out rapidly. I noticed how unwell he looked, eyes smaller, face flushed. He looked trapped. It seemed too much to hope he was innocent. "The investigation didn't take a month; I confessed a week after it happened—"

"What did you do with the money?" Garrett interrupted. Let's get to the important stuff.

"I bought a car." They all snickered. I saw an image of Mike going by me on his way to school the week before, pedaling his bike furiously with traffic in a hazy, soaking rain. I had added it to my list of reasons he was an amazing kid; he even biked to school each day. Now I was confused.

Mike was eager to go on with his story, "The manager knows me; he wanted to drop the charges when he found out it was me, but they wouldn't let him. Now I have to pay back two thousand dollars by June 11 or I get seven years in jail. It's a class A felony—"

"Sell the car," Garrett jumped in.

"I wrecked it," Mike replied. The class roared in disbelief.

"You're screwed, man," Brian shook his head.

"I know. I went to the bank with my mom yesterday to try and get a loan, but she doesn't have any credit, so we need a co-signer. And besides, if I take out a loan now, it'll screw up my college loans."

"Seven years?" Peter stared at him.

"That's what they said," Mike looked on the brink of throwing up. "But we're going to have a huge graduation party and charge everyone five dollars at the door to raise the money. We'll use a community center building."

"Are you going to have beer?" Dylan called out. Always looking for the action.

"No, chem-free," he said. The class complained loudly.

"No one's going to go," Garrett assured him. He was always straight to the point. He didn't waste his time trying to make people feel good; he went to the heart of things.

"Have a couple of kegs, man," Dylan continued.

"Wait," I said, "you don't see a problem with throwing a party with alcohol as an underaged person?" They laughed. "I think he's in enough trouble already." Mike offered a small smile. He was tensely sitting at the edge of his seat. He wanted to jump out of his skin. "Back to research, guys. Today in class . . . " I noticed Mike was a little relieved to face forward, away from the incredulous looks of the others. My heart sank with the reality of what would come. He was weeks from graduation.

Contrary to reason, the students who have fought hard to wear the cap and gown sometimes crumple in the final turn. The emotional collapse comes as the end nears, and it is a scramble to finish. I always say, *You're so close, how can you risk failing at this point?* But life can seem quite a bit scarier than the halls of high school. Some know they aren't ready. I have no idea if this is what happened with Mike; I can't imagine I could understand precisely what he was thinking when he broke into the store late one night with his friend. It wasn't hard to catch him; he had quit the job just months before. When his friends were questioned days later, he panicked and confessed. He hoped it would make things easier on him. It may have.

Mike stopped coming to school regularly. Absences accumulated like mosquitoes in spring; they had a sting. If it continued, he wouldn't graduate. He asked one day, "What day is graduation?"

I replied, "June 15."

He said anxiously, "No, June 7." I knew he needed to be right.

"No," I answered, "it really is the 15th." He looked away. The scheduled arraignment was June 11.

I stopped his friend Cody on his way out the door the next day. Cody seemed a little lost. Cody and Mike always worked together when they could; I knew that they supported each other. I asked Cody to come after school, so we could work on some of his writing. He agreed. I had to work with what I had. Cody needed help; he was often bewildered in class. He told me his mind wandered. I could explain in detail what I was looking for in a writing task, then watch almost all begin, except for Cody. Often Mike would whisper a second set of directions his way, or show him tricks on the computer when we were in the lab. One time Cody remained staring at a blank page for at least ten minutes as others started. Mike was consumed with his own work and Cody wouldn't ask for help. I thought he might be thinking, but I wanted to check. As I went by his desk I said, "Can I help you get started, Cody?"

He said, "I'm not doing it," arms crossed, eyes narrowed at me. The class looked up, anticipating a showdown. I sat at the desk next to him and wrote on the paper, *Are you really refusing to do this or do you not understand?* He wrote carefully next to my words: *I'm lost. I'm almost always lost in my classes.* I quickly began talking him through the assignment in a hushed whisper. He wrote willingly; the earlier defiance was simply a mask for his confusion. But Cody depended on Mike's companionship, and with Mike absent, he did little. I was frustrated that I could lose them both.

Mike returned. He had been working, trying to raise restitution. I was relieved that he was back; I also wanted to rescue him. I told my husband I was tempted to bail him out with a check from our savings account. Ninety percent of me wanted to, 10 percent said I'd be crazy. However well I believed I knew Mike, I didn't know everything. This was his journey, not mine. The trouble with teaching is I get too close to kids who need help. I want to offer them my guidance and my understanding, and once in awhile, my cash. I've made it a policy that I won't loan out more than lunch money, but sometimes it is hard to live with.

May 31st and Mike had a thousand dollars. His friend loaned him five hundred. He said he was now taking donations. He was working like a fiend. There was a lesson in that. He might still make it to college in the fall. Mike's determination might again overcome the temptation to crash and quit trying. He'd been here before. He had almost quit school a number of times, but he had battled back. The demons that haunted him, told him to be reckless and untamed, could be quieted. It was slow, steady work, but he was making progress.

He wrote in his journal, "I'm thinking of just taking the money and driving to Mexico before the arraignment." I answered with a long letter about making things worse, eventually having to face up to things to get back to America, and my faith that he would still make it to college. A student he barely knew in our class handed him ten dollars. Mike brought me the graduation practice schedule and showed me he'd miss practice on the day he had to go to court. He asked if he could miss practice and still graduate. I hoped he could; I hoped he would leave court that day. We both knew he might not.

We were studying *The Great Gatsby* in class. The kids marveled at the money that characters play with so freely. In one lesson I brought in an editorial on welfare reform and an article on lottery winners that end up miserable and we talked about wealth in our society. I had them draw from a hat slips of paper with dollar amounts that they could dream of spending freely in their journal. The first student drew, then said, "I only got two thousand dollars!"

Mike said, "I'd take that," his words heavy with longing. The class laughed and he grinned a little. Cody drew ten thousand dollars and he planned a pig roast for all of his friends, one night of excess. There was a simple line at the end that said he would loan money to Mike as well. He was not the only student that made the offer that day.

Mike was not a bad kid. I think in the past when I read about crime in the paper, I always assumed the kids deserved to be caught and that facing the consequences would be good for them. All of that may have been true in this case, but I saw crime and punishment differently through Mike's eyes. Mike had been struggling his whole life. He had made bad decisions during that struggle, but we all have. He wrote about the robbery one day in class. It was a series of stupid choices he had made with a friend. It had seemed harmless, the adrenalin was pumping, and he had regretted it almost the minute it was over. But there was no going back. He had tried to do the right thing by confessing, and he was very willing to repay the money, he just couldn't raise it in that limited time frame while trying to graduate from high school. I believed him. I hoped the judge would give him one more break.

June 11th arrived with a flood of sunshine. I was out of the house early on my way to Concord for a meeting, but I was thinking of Mike. By the time I was back in Conway, no one was at school and the courthouse was closed. The next day I asked our police resource officer what had happened and he didn't know, but he called over to the courthouse for me. He couldn't get an answer. My daughter's birthday, my niece's graduation, and family visiting from the West filled the week. I asked my students and no one had seen him. I kept hoping I'd run into Mike, but Saturday morning, as the rain poured from the sky, I dressed for graduation not knowing.

It was thankfully a short wait.

Mike was in the second pair to enter the gymnasium. His tassel swung as he walked, a smile never fading as he marched all the way to his seat. I was so relieved it was almost too much, with *Pomp and Circumstance* coursing through the gym and so many parents, grandparents, and friends blotting their eyes as our proud graduates filed past. Later the valedictorian thanked teachers who believed in kids even when they didn't deserve it, and Mike looked back and winked at me.

Just one wink.

I'm still smiling.

writing with teachers

As writers we are always exploring what happens, what comes next,
turning it over, finding words to sit in like chairs. . . . because words
shape the strange sorrows we are living in, help us connect.

—Naomi Shihab Nye

Eben started it.

He sent out a note about beginning a writing group for teachers. Problem was, no one could read it; Eben has the worst handwriting of anyone I know. Enough of us asked him to explain, I guess, because at our first meeting there were four English teachers, pens and notebooks ready. He chose this god-awful time of 6:30 on Friday mornings, but we went anyway.

I was curious. Eben had that writer look about him: shaggy brown hair and pleated khakis, looked like he lived on coffee and cigarettes, packed away in a small apartment building. I had been on the hiring committee and knew Eben had done graduate work at the University of New Hampshire. That name alone makes me shudder . . . the Mount Rushmore of writing with Don Graves, Don Murray, Tom Newkirk, and Jane Hansen carved across a gray granite shelf. Eben could undoubtedly teach me something.

I loved writing; in fact, I had dreamed of being an author as a child. I just never had time for it, never wrote anything except checks and sporadically in a private journal I've kept since college. I listened when Nancie Atwell said teachers should learn to write themselves in order to teach students how to write. Problem was, almost all writing teachers I knew were too busy deciphering student drafts and editing them, reading short stories and novels to use in class, and never writing any-thing themselves except notes to parents and students. It's a harried life, believe me. Who has time to love and nurture what we teach? I thought I was ahead of the rest because I wrote journal entries with my students. I rarely crafted a piece beyond a clean rough draft, though, and that is all the difference. I knew I had been waiting for this mo-ment. It was a next step for me. It was time to become a writer.

We gathered in our cramped department office, sitting in orange, stackable chairs, the brown stain of a ceiling leak striping one wall near-by. It was winter and out the window behind us the morning light played with the silvery sheen of ice. Eben gave us a topic: morning. We wrote and wrote and then we stopped and shared. Eben's piece was a ride. I was in the car with him, wandering along the highway. I could feel the curves in the road. It was only ten or fifteen lines, but I could see it when we crested the next hill. I didn't want to share after that; I just wanted to write like him.

It was awkward to regurgitate my writing, on the spot, when I knew it wasn't much. I wasn't alone. My colleagues shifted nervously in their chairs. There was an awkward silence when one finished reading. Eben noticed and said we should all bring something we were working on to our next meeting. A deadline would force us to write, he reasoned, and then we could give each other feedback. Now there's terror for you; I had to bring something I had prepared ahead of time. I couldn't hide behind *I only had ten minutes to write and it is early and I'm tired*. I had to craft something and copy it for people.

Suddenly I had nothing to write about. I sweated over one story. Hours later it was still lurching along, with stilted transitions and little vision. I could feel a spot of panic in my stomach, reminding me that I called myself a writing teacher, but I couldn't write. I knew I could miss the next few writers' group meetings and go on hiding. No one would know. They would all believe I was just too busy; they're teachers after all. No one said I had to write, except me. But every once in awhile, one sentence would come out well, maybe two or three strung together. I could hear my voice and I liked the sound of the words I put together. It wasn't much, but it got me started.

We met in Eben's room in the basement of the school a week later, below exposed pipes painted a hideous yellow-green. There were four of us. We had lost an early convert and the principal showed up instead. Go figure. I probably invited her, but I couldn't believe she showed up, a piece of writing in one hand, her radio in the other. She was paged twice on the intercom while she tried to share her piece. She finally gave up. She never returned to our group, and I can't say I was sorry. I didn't need my boss there beside me as I learned something I was sure I should know already. I made everyone else share before me that morning so that we ran out of time for mine, but I learned a few things and took those lessons with me when I approached my piece again.

That first year we probably met six times in all. It was scarier than teaching. The best part was watching Eben's students arriving for class and watching us. We would continue prattling about the piece before us and I thought it was important that those students saw teachers haggling over leads, playing with structure and voice, quibbling over the impact individual words had. I had never seen anyone process writing like that in all of my years of schooling.

The following year we gelled as a team and began weekly meetings in my classroom: Eben, Dow, Carrie, and I. We laughed until we cried. We surprised each other, we listened and counseled each other, and tore apart our writing with confidence. I'd never had professional development like this. If Carrie dropped a piece in my box on Monday, it was like a personal challenge: was I still writing? And I'd think, *Damn, I wish I could write like her*. I'd carve out the time to write that night and discover energy for teaching my classes the following day. My pieces coached me in the moves writers make, and I was eager to share these lessons with my students. I was exhilarated.

Our writing group changed as we worked together more closely. We all wrote freely and celebrated the body of work that emerged. Carrie often noticed a word or a phrase that was just right. She used

sparkly gel pens and has beautiful handwriting that breathed enthusiasm. I loved reading her annotations. She made me want to write
more. Dow's a smart reader; he sees what's submerged in a piece.
Dow always said, "Keep working with this, definitely," as if there were
no other choice. Those comments kept me writing. Eben and Dow
wrote poetry. I stuck with narratives, but I watched their moves carefully. I learned what was important in a poem and it changed how I
teach poetry.

Their criticism stung. I didn't like it. You have to be careful when
you're correcting someone's work. I don't think I was careful enough
with my students all those years before. It was so easy to just tell them
what wasn't working and think that was helping. In writers' group I
learned quickly that compliments showed me what I could do and gave
me confidence, criticism confirmed my fears and left me frustrated.
When I confidently approached a piece to revise it, I was playful. When
I went back to one in frustration, I usually made it worse. One of my
favorite readers asks questions when he's confused by my writing. He
doesn't point out weak leads, broken paragraphs, rabbit trails. He
asks. I never feel inadequate with him. That's the teacher I want to be
for my students.

I was genuinely surprised at the time it took to write. I mean to really
write. Not the first-draft kind of stuff we're used to assigning to students and then watching them compose. I'm talking the kind of writing
that reaches a point where you want to share it with everyone you
know because you finally find the story and figure out how to tell it
well. I would spend a few hours on a piece to give to the group. After
listening to their feedback, I went home and spent hours more on revision and rethinking. And because I was determined to improve, I set up
conditions to help myself write. Sometimes I worked very early in the
morning before anyone else was up, the rising sun my only distraction.
It took hours for one story to emerge.

I can't help but think of the conditions in a classroom. If I were sur-
rounded by twenty peers, I'd get sidetracked. And even on those days

when I was focused and could ignore all those around me, I might get in thirty-five minutes of writing time in a class period. I'd need a lot more than that to reread my piece enough to see what it needed. This is why kids might need months for one piece. To hear their own nagging questions. To play with words. To delete and rewrite and start over. To make it good. I don't think we give our students enough time to make their work something they're proud of. On to the next piece. Look at this curriculum! No time to linger. Quantity. Production. Progress. Somehow we decided that four short stories is better than one rewritten four times, and it's a huge mistake.

I've learned that rewriting is more important than either the first or the last draft. It is the most difficult part. When I'm frustrated with revision, I seek distractions. Different fonts. Color. Play with the tabs across the top of the screen; suddenly I'm looking like one of my students. There's a function in Microsoft Word that I love. Each document has Properties. Under this tab is one called Statistics. I use it all the time to see how long a piece of mine is. What I've recently discovered is the information I was skimming over: Revision Number and Total Editing Time. A writer had to have put those functions in this program—I mean, who else would care? I get tremendous satisfaction looking at these statistics for some of my most troublesome pieces. "Basic Training" . . . revision number: 68. Total editing time: 663 minutes. I may be a perfectionist, or just a really lousy first-draft writer, but I don't imagine my students are that different. This piece has 41 revisions and 522 minutes of writing time so far. That's real writing. I wouldn't have believed it if I hadn't struggled through each of those revisions myself. Are our classrooms designed to allow for this deep, complex construction? The true crafting of a piece that moves a writer from one place to the next?

Writing doesn't just appear in a clean, white lab coat and gloves. It's messy. Even for the masters. I visited the library in London to see "Chapter and Verse: 1000 Years of British Literature" last summer. I wandered openmouthed from one case to the next studying rough drafts from the ages . . . Charles Dickens, Emily Brontë, Jane

Austen, J. K. Rowling. Scratch-outs, words in the margin, notes to self. Whole paragraphs x-ed out boldly. I bought postcards of this work to remind myself I'm not alone.

I've watched my son's workload in eighth grade. He writes for language arts and social studies constantly. He was sitting on his bed the other night at 10 P.M. with a notebook full of lines, his fat, orange cat curled at his feet.

"Look, Mom, I'm almost done. Only one and a half to go."

He was cranking out journal entries written in the voice of a member of the Civil War. An interesting assignment, but there wasn't a single word changed in the entire piece. Cam had page after page of first-draft writing and it was "good enough." He didn't have the time or the desire to craft it any further. Did anyone expect it, really? Perhaps all of this quantity improves his writing on some level, but it also sets him up. He believes first drafts are good enough and doesn't even really know how to revise. What if his next assignment were simply to rewrite the journals . . . to rethink and construct them. What if the expectation were to produce something he valued? We fool ourselves when we think they'll do that on their own. I know, the class couldn't cover as much content if they slowed down. Tell me that's a worthwhile trade.

In that year of the writing group, I learned risk taking and listening to my own nagging questions. I wrote about subjects I had never had the courage to address. I began seeing moments from my childhood differently. I practiced the heart of memoir: seeing past events through new eyes. My writing was raw. It was a personal risk to share so much and to keep handing over drafts that I knew weren't there yet. No wonder so many of my students choose safe topics, from favorite birthdays to vacations and sports. No wonder so many hide in fiction. Don Murray told me to go after the nagging questions in my own writing and I would solve most of the problems with a piece. He was right. The questions my writing group asked often echoed my own thinking. I started to get frustrated when Carrie would ask, "Is this really true?" and I'd think, *No. I knew that.* I wanted to find the inconsistencies myself. Revision and more revision, an endless cycle. There's not a single piece in this book that doesn't need further work in my mind. I'm always fine-tuning.

I can tell you I still cringe when someone calls me a writer. I'm not good enough for that title yet. I read Annie Dillard or Barbara Kingsolver and shake my head. It will be many years before I could hope to sit beside them. I bet our students feel that way when we hand over models of great writing: the Sharon Creech stories, the Chris Crutcher novels. Do published pieces tell them writing well is for a gifted few who somehow magically nail it all in the first draft? Only if we don't also show them the steps along the way. Only if we aren't willing to walk beside them as they try.

We need to nurture the fire that made us English teachers. We should contribute pieces to the school literary magazine or perform at the next Poetry Slam. We must process writing with our students, not stand as the authority when we are afraid to try the craft ourselves. We should give our colleagues the gift of having written, and give our students the gift of having a writer for a teacher. We have to find the time. Memoir, poetry, and short stories won't come easy for any of us, but we need the inside view of what we are asking of our students. I'm launching a research project this week in class, and I will research as well. I'm going to gather facts on note cards and struggle to tie the ideas together. I'd rather not, actually, but how will I teach this well if I don't?

Eben has moved to the Ukraine with the Peace Corps. Carrie has fallen in love and rushes home at the end of a day. Dow is buried in prep for his many high school classes and I'm an exhausted administrator. We met about once a month this year with new companions: Ed, Bonnie, and Ishi. It is tough to start again, to carve out time to meet and share and laugh. To feel close enough to risk sharing what matters to us. Our group has to find its rhythm and we lose the beat when other things get in the way.

Ed shared a piece in January that reminded me of why it is worth the effort. He brought it still warm from the Xerox machine; he'd written the draft during his last-period planning time. It was a fishing story, but a life story as well. Ed took a student out to a lake last spring, a foreign exchange student just days from heading home. They fished together and watched a rainbow dance across the water. Two days later the boy drowned. Ed's piece made us cry. I hadn't known Ed had grieved for this lost boy, a half a world from his home. I didn't know that repetition in his poem could imitate a heartbeat and course through me like the blood in my veins. I felt the power of poetry draw us together that afternoon, as clouds covered the sun and our room became cool and dark. It is why writing matters, why we must teach our students to do it well. Their lives will be filled with such stories waiting to be told.

Ours already are.

pay attention

We cannot copy others but we can discover how their craft,
processed through our own experience as people and as writers,
can improve our craft.

—Donald M. Murray

I'm a kleptomaniac; I steal every good thing I see. It is a secret to my teaching. I once told a friend, "I don't think I've ever had an original thought in my life; I just feed off of others." I read and study the methods of educators who publish their work. I attend conferences and soak in the ideas and successes of those I admire. I design lessons in my head as I watch the latest TV special on teaching. I share and borrow and adapt. Most recently I've learned to teach this to my students as well.

"Class, today I'll teach you how to steal," I begin with the direct lesson model, stating my objective clearly so they all know where we are going.

"Yes! Alright! A lesson I can actually use," Alan calls from the back row. We all laugh.

"Actually, you're right, Alan. My intention is to teach you something you will use—in your writing."

He groans.

I begin by framing the lesson with my own experiences as a writer. I write like those I admire. In the beginning I studied the work of Mitch Albom of *The Detroit Free Press*. You might know his work from his terrific book *Tuesdays with Morrie*. He has a column that I have bookmarked in my Internet organization box. I pop in regularly, skipping the columns on spoiled athletes and baseball, absorbing every word of his feature stories on life in a city I lived near for five years. Anything on the Red Wings; they are my favorite sports team of all time. I absorb his writing style as well.

Mitch taught me the weight of a fragment. I still remember stumbling over one in the first paragraph of a powerful piece, "A Deadly Decision," a column published December 31, 1997. The sentence "Early June" made me pause. I stopped and reread. I began again. The paragraph paints a scene and you don't need any more words in that sentence. A series of short phrases works to set the stage for a long column that endeavors to tell a tragic story in a limited space. I liked it. But I was instantly struck by the fact that it broke "the rules." We've taught students to avoid fragments. A sentence is a complete thought. Don't leave me hanging. *But wait a minute,* I thought, *this fragment works.*

When I share the piece with my students, I let them absorb the entire story, then draw them back to the opening paragraph. I point out how Mitch used a fragment. There is initially a euphoria on several faces. "We found an error!" Students love to turn the tables on those who correct their work. "This is a bad model, Mrs. Kittle."

"Is it?" I ask playfully.

As a class we fill in the other words that could complete the thought in that sentence, then reread the paragraph. It loses something. We try again with other fragments in the column. The fragments work better than forced complete sentences. They create a casual voice that reveals a story. Mitch's voice. It sounds similar to the voices we use ourselves in conversation. I picture my daughter and her good friend Lucy huddled together on a log, swapping stories in hushed voices after school. That is a voice that draws you near to the writer. It isn't a voice you'd choose for every genre, of course, but it is effective in many. Students need to be taught the crucial importance of using a voice that will compel readers to listen to their words.

The next exercise is to practice writing fragments. Lucky my principal hasn't arrived for an unplanned visit, huh? I ask them to play with fragments as they write a short narrative on breakfast. We start to sound an awful lot like Mitch Albom, but many like the technique. Mostly they like breaking rules.

"My fifth-grade teacher underlined every fragment I wrote, Mrs. Kittle," Stephanie smugly relates from the first row. "She stifled my writing."

"Perhaps," I offer, "but aren't there times when a fragment really is a problem for the reader?"

The class considers. Boy, I'd love to jump in here and answer my own question.

"Yes," Adam hesitates, unsure.

I wait.

"You know the sentences that start to say something and then there's a period and you're still waiting to hear the rest?" Adam is struggling to say this, forming the thoughts as he speaks. Adam battles with fragments in his own work, so I'm surprised to find him answering me.

"I think so. Could you give us an example?" I encourage him, holding out the chalk in my right hand.

Adam comes to the board. He's grown five inches this year, at least. Still awkward in his feet, he moves a bit like a golden retriever puppy. He writes, *Women should stay in the kitchen where they belong because.*

I can't believe it. Adam has a slight flush in his cheeks, but a broad smile as he hands me the chalk and absorbs the class applause. You just never know what a student is thinking. I tell him privately that the next time I see him on the ice I'll check him into the boards. He laughs.

After a brief, but predictable, gender equality lecture, I ask students to explain the distinct difference between *Early June* and Adam's example. They can feel it. Mitch captures a complete thought in two words. Ten arranged differently are just wrong. We discuss how style is one thing, but you can't make a reader work too hard or she will give up on the piece altogether. Fragments that leave a reader hanging are work. Fragments that complete a thought add balance to sentence structure but, we agree, should be used sparingly. If used too often they set up their own rhythm that could overwhelm the content.

"That's it," I say. "That's the lesson. Steal from good writers. Pay attention to what writers are up to and copy their approaches in your own work."

"But that's cheating," Nicole says quietly, not quite sure she wants me to hear. Some students wrestle with challenging their teachers. (Not enough of them, however.)

"It is if you steal their words, Nicole, you're right. Thanks for helping me clarify that. It's actually called plagiarism. But I believe if you simply model your writing after successful writers in order to tell your own stories, you're practicing a craft. I want you to consciously consider structure and technique when you read in order to improve your own writing."

We practice pilfering by examining the leads in several novels by the same author. It takes a rich classroom library to make this happen. I watch students grab books and partners and find a corner to compare together. They quickly see patterns.

"I bet this next one will start with dialogue, just like the other two," Amy says, holding the book tightly to her chest as she states her prediction publicly. Amy is always quick to move from one step to the next in her thinking. She takes risks. She opens the book and reads the lead to her group. It doesn't begin with dialogue. She is intrigued, not disappointed. The entire room is rich with thoughts on what they are discovering in the writing, beyond the story. I wander and enjoy, but I do not lead. It is my favorite kind of teaching. If we can show our students what writers are up to, their writing can begin to take shape in ways they hadn't imagined. Success will push their writing further.

Our students are imitators of all they see. I've caught a student using my voice or gestures more than once, to their regret. With writing, however, imitation has the potential for growth. We become apprentices to writing every time we read.

demolition derby

Teaching is no easy street on which we glide, roller blades in place,
toward a fast-approaching summer vacation.

—Jane Fraser

The school year explodes into activity on the very first day; you can almost see the smoke from peeling tires. Announcements, emergency cards, and lunch forms fight for your attention with many children who crowd through the door with varied expectations, wants, and needs. In those first few days, you race along just trying to keep the car on the road, but as a new teacher you're vulnerable to getting rammed from all sides.

Your room schedule changes. You will move to a different classroom second period to accommodate a newly enrolled handicapped student. You can't imagine how you will transport your materials and get to class on time. It is the first of many jolts to come.

There are 20 copies of the book you want to teach and you have 24 students. Your department chairman has no funds to buy you additional copies. Do you abandon the text you had chosen and had begun to develop a passion for, or seek another title? You have 120 dusty copies of something else. Wonder why. Do you break down and purchase four copies yourself? Decision made, back to driving.

A side slam by the department of education, who will not approve certification earned in another state. What is required to get certified will take hours to complete and must be done by March or the district will not renew your contract. The paperwork is left on the left side of the desk and you maneuver back into traffic, but you can feel it behind you. Like a police cruiser in your rearview mirror, you can't quite get it out of your mind.

Angry parent phone call. The parent went straight to your principal, whom you've barely spoken to since the year began. His secretary asks you to stop by on your free period. You wait in line for fifteen minutes to speak to him, regretting you haven't brought some of the papers you need to grade, sweat forming as you listen to the phones ringing in the main office. Each one could be another call about you. Finally he is free. He listens to your plans and a brief description of your assessment tools and offers his support. He seems like a good guy. Back on the road.

The clock in the department office is off by five minutes and no one mentioned it to you, so you're late to your next-period class. Insolent students are in the halls when you arrive harried. Gathering them together takes too long, the lesson isn't going well, your teaching is flat. You watch the rolled eyes, hear their sighs, feel their boredom. The timing is off all period; there is no spark in the eyes of your students today.

You've finally survived the first month of teaching, only to discover that progress reports are due in two days. You haven't done a lot of thinking about how you will assess your students in all areas and you haven't put grades in the computer yet. You decide to write extensive commentary on each progress report, not realizing that the process will take eight hours. Do you abandon the plan even though you know it is the right thing to do? Your authentic assessment dreams feel anything but at this point. It all sounded so good in college, but now it feels impossible to put together. You had hoped to take a break this weekend.

The faculty meeting has been rescheduled for this afternoon and you had planned to pick up groceries after school. You'll be late again and are frustrated with how this job has consumed you. You are completely spent when you get home at the end of a day. You go to bed earlier than ever now and still awake tired.

You find a note in your mailbox you weren't expecting. You've been scheduled for a formal observation with the assistant principal, whom you haven't met. You need to bring your plans to her office tomorrow. This feels like a crash, but you convince yourself there is nothing to worry about. She seems nice enough and likes your plan. You rehearse the lesson numerous times that evening and early the next morning. The class is flawless, but the assistant principal doesn't show. You try to hide your frustration. She appears on time for your next class, a rowdy group, stays for thirty minutes, and leaves without saying a word.

You are staggered by a morning announcement. The soccer team has made the district tournament and players will be dismissed forty-five minutes early to attend the game. You had scheduled the test for the last part of the day, which means you'll have to write an alternate test tonight to give to those students and plan something independent for the rest of the class to do while they take it. Forget the introduction to the next unit and your plans for an interactive technology experience. Rescheduling your time in the writing lab will be tough, but putting off the test would be worse.

A student is waiting for you when you arrive at the room. She complains vehemently about her grade on the research paper. You were sure it was plagiarized and even asked three colleagues to take a look at it, but no one was familiar with the student, so it was your judgment call. It looks like you made the wrong call, but you just feel in your gut that you didn't. The student is seething when she leaves the class. Another phone call will probably follow.

The cold air greets you when you open your classroom door. Fifty-seven degrees because the heat is not working in your portable class-room. Students are freezing. The principal relocates your class to the library. You feel your car sliding into reverse. Not only will you be on display in a space used by many students and staff, but you can't *teach* here. What will you do with them? You have three minutes to decide.

A fire drill interrupts the first productive discussion you've managed this week. Your teachable moment is lost. Those teachable moments are hard to find any way. They are the moments promised to you in teacher education. It is tough to get the students back on track once you return to class. Several are late, unreasonably so. You feel taken advantage of.

Lunch is hot dogs or beef stroganoff . . . both look and smell horrible. You didn't have time to pack anything this morning and you're starving. While you're wandering around the cafeteria, one table begins to playfully toss pretzels at each other. Ignore it or not? It escalates. Two begin wrestling, punches are thrown, you look around and see that you are the only adult in the room besides the cafeteria workers. The students are watching you. You step in. Halting this battle and taking the students to the office, filling out discipline referrals and regaining your composure consume the minutes left in lunch. You're still hungry and hope you put an energy bar in your desk drawer as you scramble down the hall to your classroom.

Students late to class. You demand they get a tardy slip from the office. They protest; you are the only teacher that counts students tardy within one minute of the bell. You're unfair. The entire class, it seems, joins in the discussion. These students have challenged you in front of the whole class and you think you must stand firm. You send them to the office and turn to face the rest of the class, anger traveling like waves across the space between you. What was your lesson today?

You purchased a classroom set of newspapers to use in a four-week unit designed around the presidential campaign. It is a fair rate, but comes out of your pocket. For days you wait and finally see your name attached to a stack of papers left at the front door. Triumphant, you take them to your room and watch for twenty-five minutes as every student pores through the paper. At the end of the reading time you ask how many carry a daily newspaper at home and not a single hand goes up. Buoyed by the obvious need for the papers, you leave the house early the next day to be sure to scoop them up before class and do a little pre-reading. They aren't there. Two days later and still no papers.

You call the *Globe*. They delivered them. That means someone took them . . . ? Would another teacher do that? Your plea to teachers at the faculty meeting provides no answers and no papers. Your students are frustrated, your plans are in the toilet, and your money seems to be supplying someone else with classroom materials. Some mornings it is more than you can stand.

You pull your car over to the side of the road and stay home to sleep late, rethink your career choice, and nip this cold you feel starting in your throat. You manage to catch up on laundry, be inspired by *Oprah!* and think little about your classroom until the evening. You awake refreshed and arrive early to pull out a pile of memos, announcements, and phone messages from your main office mailbox. Scribbled across your plans are notes from the substitute. You read:

> This is the worst class I have ever been assigned to in thirty-three years of classroom teaching. Your students were disrespectful and rude. John, Brad, Justin, Sylvia, and Aaron had to be sent to the principal and Aaron did not return to class after lunch. I abandoned your plans and had the department chairman locate a video for the afternoon. Do not request me to substitute for you again.

You feel the heat in your cheeks as you thrust the note to the bottom of the paperwork and head down the hall. You are greeted warmly by students waiting at your classroom door. An unexpected fuel injection: they missed you! The day is so smooth and enjoyable, you are tempted to dismiss the first three months of the year. The students work, they compare you favorably with your substitute, and they laugh at your jokes. Your shoulders relax. Teaching is such great work.

The afternoon mail contains test results from the state certification exam. You missed the cutoff by six points. Impossible. You remember composing your piece for the exam with an attention to detail and style that most adults are incapable of. Passing this test was one thing you were sure of, and it cost you eighty dollars! It will take another eighty dollars to retake the test in two months, plus a trip to Boston, 160 miles away. Failure to pass the test by spring will cost you your job. You decide to challenge the results, convinced there has been an error. You spend an hour on the phone and another composing a letter to challenge the test before you reheat pizza for dinner. This just isn't fair.

You are motoring along, trying to maintain momentum in your unit, feeling the key elements pulling together. It is December and your colleague warns you: *Curves ahead, slow your speed to the holiday pace.* You ignore her. You have purposeful work planned for every day until vacation and it fits nicely together. It is easy to shrug off unsolicited advice when you have a detailed road map before you. Monday brings an ice storm: late opening. It's just a speed bump. The classes are shortened, but you condense the work and keep moving. Two days later school is cancelled due to a snowstorm. It's a marvelous day of leisure, but you spend some of it scrambling to reassemble your unit, shuffling the activities among the boxes in your plan book. Problem is, when the students return, they only want to talk and write about snow. It is like listening to a buzzing under your dashboard as you're driving, an annoyance you avoid dealing with until the hum makes you just a little crazy.

Rest area ahead: winter vacation. Reflective time. You realize how often this fall you've been lost in the dark. Teaching can be such an unfamiliar road. You've been following maps drawn by someone else, trying to implement curriculum that you don't always see the importance of. You feel the loneliness of a long drive. Days can disappear without interaction with another adult in the building. You stay late and arrive early and eat lunch at your desk. Something has to change or you'll be looking for an exit ramp.

January brings the close of another quarter. Student and parent complaints about grades. One in particular is your fault: a miscalculation. It is like being pulled over by the flashing blue and red lights. Your gut hurts, your head spins, you can't quite defend yourself properly as you watch other drivers slow down to see what all the excitement is about. The parent implies you need to go back to driving school. You collapse in tears after she leaves.

It occurs to you that what you need is a good mechanic, someone who knows your particular model and can anticipate problems. Someone who can clear the windshield or help you overhaul the transmission after you've pushed the pedal too far to the floor. You know just whom to call. The English teacher down the hall has the experience. Her car may be worn and a little battered, but she has a high blue book value. She agrees to help. She has always wanted to mentor a young teacher. It is like going in for repairs; she seems to know how to fix everything at once. Buoyed by her confidence, you start again.

March arrives with the whisper of spring. Students are restless, but your fine-tuning has made a difference. Your transitions are quick, power windows instead of the hand-crank version you began with in September. You can move students from group work back to a whole-class discussion in two minutes or less. The assistant principal pops in for a visit and sees this in action. You feel good.

You notice the headline on local schools in the paper on the way out of the grocery store and anxiously read it over your dinner that evening. A group of Concerned Citizens is challenging the school budget. One calls your school an "illiterate cesspool." Teacher salaries are questioned. The test scores aren't high enough. You feel the weight of public distrust descend on your tight shoulders. No one cares how hard you have been working; it isn't hard enough.

The testing service rejects your appeal and you must retake the exam. You are insulted and fuming, but you sign up for the April test and cough up another eighty dollars. It is criminal. You're beginning to feel a bit like a crash test dummy, tossed from one thing to the next.

April brings tulips and sunshine. The budget passes easily in an evening election. Student attitudes improve. Your mentor leaves M&M's in your mailbox to remind you of your meeting in the afternoon. You realize what a difference her support has meant on your journey this year; her guidance has been your in-dash global positioning system. You hear her voice in your head when a lesson starts to veer offtrack and quickly shift gears to change the pace. She is your hero.

The standardized tests eat away at two weeks of teaching and leave you breathless. May arrives with a heavy dose of spring fever. The tops come down on cars all over the road, and unfortunately, in your classroom. You read the school dress code and require girls arriving in tiny shirts to find one that will cover their bellies and everything else they display so willingly. You question the length of their skirts and shorts, earning the disgust of your students. "We thought you were cool," rings in your ears as you head home that night. Why must everything be so difficult?

The test results are in the afternoon mail. You passed. This is the jump start you needed. You plan happily for the final weeks of the school year, confident your car will have a place in the school parking lot again next fall. You are nearing the end of a challenging journey and slow to appreciate the sights along the way. Your students have matured and changed; their challenges are less frequent and with much less fire than early in the year. Your colleagues have become familiar road signs, some cherished rest stops, and others just more experienced drivers that unintentionally cut you off when you're trying to make progress. You're ready for a rest, a little more battered than when you began, but running smoothly and ready for the years ahead.

The stre...

e...

reasonable response, she heard a
"This is so-o-o boring," and seve...
"That's inappropriate. You h...
opposition quickly, she tho...
the need to be Teache...
scanned the room. Q...
warning. The ones
been cautioned
stance and st...
gin; I'm tou...
Warn...
Wa...

I have to...
scious o...
teachers. If you give...
done that's worse, so that makes me ...
ally amazed by the moves teachers make when co...
of teaching, it is easy for me to forget how difficult it is to learn u... ,
on your feet every day.

New teachers sometimes have a precarious, hesitant hold on discipline. They can be too distracted by the complexities of lesson design to focus on minor skirmishes, the harbingers of serious confrontation. Some create a discipline plan, but it is lost in a moment of frustration and they become the Teacher in Charge at any cost. The way back to a positive classroom environment can seem hopelessly tangled with weeds. And everyone in the room is watching. Schools have to have supports in place for new teachers so an episode like the following doesn't begin an end to a career.

This conflict began when her lesson started to unravel. "Why do we have to study Cro-Magnon man?" someone called from the back row. Miss James wasn't sure she could answer; someone at the state had mandated this curriculum and she had been working daily to summon the enthusiasm needed to teach it. Before she could formulate a

...voice call from across the room.
...al others sighed in response.
..._ave a warning," she glared. _Squelch the_
..._ught; it is just a matter of resolve._ She felt
..., before things got out of hand. Her eyes
...ell those conversations in the back row with a
...who hoot at that get a warning as well. She had
...that students would test her, so she fortified her
...eeled herself for battle. Let the discipline drumbeat be-
..._gher than you are._
...ng.
...rning.
Detention.
Warning.

A steady rhythm rose. The students were persistent and some even seemed to enjoy it. More than half the class was facing detention before things began to settle, but it did indeed stop, and that inspired her a little. After all, she was beginning to falter there in the middle, but she stuck to her guns and they settled down. She was in control.

She took a breath. Things were going to be fine until she saw Cindy in the back row. She'd been trouble since the first day. Always contrary. She challenged everything with her eyes and a toss of her bleached blonde ponytail. She was Trouble. It was Cindy's smirk that forced this young teacher to draw the line; students were not going to laugh at her.

"The next one who smiles gets a detention," she spat, the words flung like darts across cluttered desks. She had seemed so sweet; it was hard to believe she had suddenly narrowed her eyes threateningly at them. Several students inhaled and pushed their backs against their chairs. They were amused. _Time for the show; this will definitely be more fun than World History._ She could feel the room change as students sat up straighter, planning strategy. Oh no. A few cowered behind the person in front of them, but only a few. These kids weren't scared.

Miss James reconsidered. This was a mistake. This would be a great moment to backtrack, say "just kidding" and laugh, but they'd see right through it. They'd know she'd lost her nerve. They wouldn't take her seriously if she caved in now. She had no time to consider her choices carefully; all eyes were on her. Miss James decided to stand her ground.

No smiling.

You can guess what happened next. Cindy waited to catch Miss James' eye, then pulled her lips back to show all of her teeth as she mumbled something. Miss James couldn't quite hear her, but she assumed the worst when students nearby giggled into their hands.

Detention!

Cindy called out emphatically, "I'm not going to detention for *smiling*," making the words sound so ridiculous Miss James began to feel nauseous. The class nodded; a few clapped. Snickers raced from desk to desk. Miss James felt the sweat gathering at her hairline, a blush in her cheek. It was a giant trap she'd tumbled into; the jaws were near. This was not a battle she ever thought she would be fighting, and truthfully she wanted to retreat, she just had no idea how.

I imagine Cindy was fighting for all the collected injustices of the last eleven years of her schooling—teachers who didn't listen, the grades she didn't like, the feeling of being so small in a room of other voices— but most likely, that wasn't it at all. Miss James was just a stone in Cindy's shoe—a constant irritation. Miss James misspelled words on the board. She couldn't find her lecture notes. She didn't seem to know all that much about world history. And damn, she was young. Cindy just didn't want to tolerate being taught by a beginner. She was an honors sophomore and she deserved better.

There would be no winners here.

Miss James pulled out the heavy artillery. She had to do something; Cindy was refusing to follow her rules. She hit the button for the main office and said calmly, "I need the principal in my room." Everyone stopped. A few boys murmured, "Ooooo Cindy," but it was subdued. The principal meant business. We weren't dealing with the infantry anymore; the general was coming. Miss James was relieved when the class waited quietly.

The principal arrived quickly and saw folded arms, the defiant stares, felt the tension pulsing in the room. He unconsciously adjusted his tie, feeling it was a little tight against his neck. With a quick look around, he recognized the class president, several members of the soccer team, the honor roll. This wasn't quite what he had expected. Miss James explained that a student was refusing to serve detention and she wanted him to clarify that a refusal to attend detention would result in suspension. She was trembling.

The silence was serious.

He scanned the room again, thinking. This was a test of *his* vision for the school and its students, and he must consider his options cautiously. He was determined to help his new teachers, but he wished he'd stayed in his office. He said suspension can depend on the circumstances, of course; he would need to hear both sides. Cindy smiled broadly. Miss James quickly drew a breath; how would she defend this rule against smiling? She could feel her students sitting up taller, relishing victory. This wasn't the support she was looking for. She was crushed. And still she must return to teaching as the principal made his exit.

Miss James could't believe she was here, in this moment, after all she went through to become a teacher. She had worked several jobs and paid her way through college, determined to make a difference with kids. She was nervous, but so excited to set up her own classroom. She had painted the room, cleaned out cupboards, given up hours of time to prepare for the year, but the students ignored her hard work and simply scowled at her assignments and defied her rules. It wasn't fair; she thought her youth would be an asset instead of a weakness. She wanted desperately to be an effective teacher, but the path there wasn't marked clearly. Until today, Miss James had been nervously holding her own, mostly enjoying the challenges of becoming a teacher. Few students had confronted her; most had been pleasant. She would admit she was clambering to learn an effective planning model that would keep her classroom running smoothly, but until now she'd avoided this kind of public showdown.

But if it was going to happen, she knew it would happen here. There was something about *this* class. They seemed poised to keep her scrambling, making her anxious as they filed in through the door each day. Everything was harder with this class; they seized any opportunity to make her stumble. Today in the space of ten minutes she had moved from teacher to lieutenant. She could feel it: infamy. She'd be known throughout the school for one thing: she gives detentions for smiling. Despair quickly overpowered her resolve.

Would she surrender? How would she return to teaching if she did?

No learning will occur in an environment of hostility where students are determined to see a teacher fail. This battle is destined to become a war, and new teachers are seldom prepared to lose. It won't be easy for Miss James, but with guidance from an experienced, understanding teacher, she'll be able to face her students the next day. It won't be as hard as she thinks. The trouble is, in too many buildings all over this country, there is no money for the mentoring of new teachers. Our rookies are all alone out there and a scene like this one can snowball into an early exit from the career. I've watched it happen. I won't forget the teacher my colleague found clinging to the chalkboard tray with both hands as the class exploded in chaos around him. He quit the next week.

Classroom management is really about the management of the heart and soul of your students. The only "technique" that works is a full-hearted human response to their lives, and to the conditions of school. In some schools students sit in rows and listen, then rush to their next class, to sit and listen even more. Try to understand the conditions in your particular school and view the entire day through their eyes. Shadow a student for a day. I'm serious. Try making the number of transitions we require of them in seven hours and see if you don't burn out at some point and begin writing a note to a friend. This doodling and boredom rarely has much to do with the teacher. You aren't bad. Your students are children, preoccupied with myriad distractions. It is a natural state. School is often the unnatural one.

Miss James needs to know her students and they need to know her. If you don't connect to students, they listen less, trust you less, and learn less. And I promise you this: most do not want to see you fail. But they want a voice in the classroom and you must learn how to hear it, without being threatened by it.

You must teach the students, not the content. I want every student in my class to know that he or she is more important than what I am teaching. Just this week I learned that a student who has been testing me daily has never had his mother in his life. He has been leaving for fifteen minutes on a bathroom pass, then arriving dramatically while I'm addressing the class. There are twenty-eight other students in my room and so I have been putting out these little fires, but missing the embers that remain. I need to halt the pattern we've established of his disobedience and my response. It isn't going to go away. I began asking questions of my colleagues. What's the story of this kid? It didn't take long to find one who remembered Brian well. Now I'm armed with the knowledge I need to change my reactions to him and redirect his behavior positively.

Plan for group time so that you can move around the room, listening to student conversations about the content and noticing how they respond to their peers. I work with a colleague who has his high school students create a map as a group activity to build community in the first week of school. Each map has to contain the house of each person in the group and ten landmarks from our valley of towns. It is an activity in problem solving and collaboration and allows Ed the opportunity to circle around the groups and learn about his students. Casual conversations pay big dividends.

Be in your room before and after class to chat. Make eye contact with every student every day. At least make it a goal. Share your homemade cookies. Laugh. Be approachable. Ask your colleagues, school guidance counselors, and coaches about your students. Attend sporting events and musical performances. Eat lunch in the cafeteria. Chaperone a dance. Stand in the hall between classes. You won't get paid for many of these things, but the payoff for knowing your students is powerful. It is one of the lasting joys of teaching. You'll find yourself cheering every single one of them on. You'll dread that last day of the year when your time together ends. You'll look across a classroom of faces and know the stories that hide behind baseball caps and body piercings, and not only will it make management easier, it will keep you coming back every year. The students were the reason you chose this profession, and knowing them will keep you in it. You can begin to make a difference in their lives if you know what their lives are all about.

It won't be seamless, face-forward, eyes-on-teacher teaching and it won't work all of the time. I make mental adjustments to my management plan every year when I meet my students. Today Jeff began class huddled under the hood of his sweatshirt, splayed across his desk, eyes shut. I told him he couldn't sleep and he barely opened his eyes to acknowledge me. I asked him a question and he pulled his head up off the desk and opened his book while Alan said, "Geez, Mrs. Kittle, he's tired. Leave him alone." I was tempted, but I couldn't set that example for the class. When it came time to work with partners, he took his chair and moved outside of the classroom, slamming the door behind him. I gave him a minute and then followed him outside. Forty degrees. Damn these portable classrooms. I expected him to be sitting with his arms folded, glaring at me. Jeff was writing, doing the work I had asked partners to complete together. He wasn't being defiant; he needed space. I could see him struggling to connect to our novel. I crouched near him and said, "How can I help you?"

Tears instantly appeared. I know a little of his story: a court date last week, moving out of his mother's house . . . I don't know what else. If I push him, he'll give up. He owes several assignments at the moment. If I stick to a penalty for each day the work is late, he'll fail. We talked and he said he couldn't do any work tonight. He had to move his things.

After I listened he said he would try to complete the work. I left him and returned to class. He came inside before the end of class with his journal and asked for the work he had missed earlier in the week. I wasn't sure if he would do it, but he might. If I had forced him to comply and work with a partner, or even in the classroom for that matter, today would have been lost. We'd be headed for a battle. If I accepted the conditions he needed today, I'd get more out of him on the days he can contribute. Today Jeff needed my understanding more than my knowledge of English. I had to make a management plan just for him. It is the real, everyday work of teaching; there are no shortcuts.

These accommodations for students frustrate me at times. Attending to the needs of an individual can take me away from the discussion or the momentum I'm trying to build in the class, and sometimes I react badly. But those moments, if played well, can let my students know I'll treat them with respect, listen, and help them be successful. That is my most powerful teaching tool. I'd rather they all arrived "ready to learn," interested in an examination of the role of American culture in American literature. I drool at the thought of how much teaching I could do. I think English is fascinating, but they're teenagers after all. Some days they are just here to play the game of school and move on to the rest of their lives. And my mission is not just to teach English, I must teach empathy and tolerance, forgiveness and compassion, when most of our culture preaches something else entirely. To do that, I position myself to avoid daily battles and win that war.

A former student stopped me in the hall this week to say hello and mentioned the latest skirmish in Miss James' class. Almost every student has refused to speak for two days. On the first day, one shy voice answered from the edge of the room but the others stared at Miss James, lips sealed. A tenth-grade ground war—nobody move. And we say teenagers have no discipline. I listened, but told Nick that he wouldn't earn any medals for this one. I told him there are other ways to resolve a conflict with a teacher and I encouraged him to halt the attack. This class is trying to get back at Miss James, determined to win something.

This year is simply the first draft of Miss James' teaching. This snapshot I've shown you is not the teacher she wants to be. Students like Cindy and Nick, however, will help her revise her understanding of her role in the class and in the lives of her students. She must make the same effort to know them as people as she makes to understand her subject. This battle is really not with her students as much as with herself. With guidance, she will learn what is worth fighting for. Without it, she may choose something less threatening to do to earn a living. I left Miss James a note, because together we can figure out a cease-fire. Like a good editor, I can help Miss James rewrite this class. Eventually when her students smile, it will be a measure of her success, instead of the enemy flashing their teeth.

" Treat every student the same by treating each one differently "

watching Joe

Our students watch every move we make.
They know what we value by what we do.

—Linda Rief

I've read it a thousand times: it's the teacher. No other factor has more impact on learning than being in the hands of an accomplished teacher. One study says the impact is twenty times greater than any other factor in student achievement. We don't need numbers to tell us this. If my own children love their teachers, the year is filled with lightness and joy. Projects are adventures; learning is natural and lasting. If they don't like a teacher, it is a stone dropped into a pond. The first ripple is their hatred of the subject, the second their refusal to try, the third a general malaise that colors time before and after school. The teacher matters.

Today I went to Joe's first-period class, an honors section of American Literature. It is a mixture of juniors and seniors. This is the education people dream of for their children: sixteen students in a comfortable room, natural light from a bank of windows along one wall, focused, meaningful work, and a teacher like Joe.

Joe laughs and talks with students as they trickle in from homeroom. Taylor has just returned from Cuba for spring vacation and brought Joe a straw hat and a pound of coffee. High school students rarely surprise teachers with presents. Joe puts it on his head, transforming his look into fisherman. He laughs as they do. He doesn't take attendance; he doesn't have to. He knows with a glance around the room who is missing. In our school we work hard to limit class size. We believe it is critical to educating our students well. I know there are places in Florida and California where even in the eighth grade, the numbers have crept up to forty or more. I've met teachers at national conferences who spoke of working among this mass of adolescence. It isn't the education a small, intimate time with a teacher can be. It isn't even close. And yes, I know some students will continue to learn and excel even in a class of forty, but more will not.

Joe loves baseball. He volunteers his time coaching because he was hired long after the present coach began his reign, but Joe just can't stay away once April arrives. He throws with the pitchers before the snow melts. Joe is passionate about the Red Sox; he is about life. He cross-country skis in the dark with just the light of a headlamp to help him through the trees. He has created a website with his poetry on it for students to visit and consider. Joe is convincing, likable, and a true student of literature.

It is mid-April and students are still preoccupied with the March Madness basketball tourneys. Joe taps into their interest and introduces his class to the Poetry Sweet Sixteen. Joe has sixteen poems from the Harlem Renaissance, eight to a side, and the poems will square off round after round until one is declared the winner, based on a class average score on a rubric. Joe has married his love for sports with his love for poetry in this project. Kids have read the poems the night before and done their own rankings to determine a winner. Joe collects these as they write in journals about the winning choice. Now that students have invested a little of themselves, Joe begins to lead the class through a calculated discovery of the inner and outer meanings in these poems. The key here is *leads*. Discovery teaching. Joe does not present himself as the authority of this work; he does not lecture. He does not present his interpretation, nor dictate his favorites. He asks for students to defend their own likes and dislikes and then he augments their understanding with his.

It works like this: First he puts the students in groups based on a playing card he passed to each as they wrote in journals. Joe puts students in close proximity with those they wouldn't choose to work with in order for them to see another point of view. But Joe also throws out a wild card. One student has a king, which means she can choose to work wherever she wants. A little choice, a little luck of the draw, and no one complains.

Each group is given a poem to talk about so that they can be the experts on that poem during discussion. After ten minutes of group discussion the class work begins. The first seed in the tournament is read aloud boisterously by a student volunteer. Joe asks, "Who will defend this poem? Who will tell us why it should move on to the next round?" Students are eager to highlight strengths. When one answers, Joe replies, "Can anyone add to what she has said?" Four do. Joe is skillful at scaffolding student responses, one after another, to strengthen the reasoning, the listening, and the respect students have for each other.

"Who has a weakness?" Joe is ready to move the group forward.

"This poem is choppy," Tess says.

"Do you mean the rhythm?" Joe asks.

"Yeah, it isn't even, all the way to the end," she replies.

Joe explains to the whole class that there are two kinds of rhythm in a poem, either controlled or frenzied, and each creates a mood. With a few sentences of instruction, Tess takes off, explaining that the poet is growing more frustrated, even angry, as the poem moves on and that is why the tempo changes. Tess has discovered what is happening in this poem. She has made the leap to thinking about the poet's intentional use of varied rhythm with Joe's careful guidance. She is certainly reading with more insight than when class started. But this is a far different result than if Joe had simply lectured the class on the use of rhythm in this Langston Hughes' poem. Tess might have been daydreaming, "Yeah, whatever," as Joe explained. When instead he says, "Do you think Hughes might have used this varied rhythm for an intentional effect?" Tess has the chance to discover the answer herself. That empowers her. Teachers with all of the answers make students feel frustrated, stupid, and unwilling to try. Teachers who say, "I think you can bring something to the reading of the poem that will help all of us to understand," value the intelligence of their students and get much better results. Especially when Joe responds to a student, as he does later in this lesson, "I never thought of that before; I missed that completely."

I'm not advocating that teachers quit teaching. Joe is particularly skillful at blending his advanced understanding of American literature with his students' limited exposure to it. But his stance is never *Come to the fountain of knowledge and drink.* That arrogance makes teenagers crazy. Rather, *Let us share and learn from each other. We journey together and I am your guide.*

Casey, a brilliant thinker, says, "Mr. Fernald, you know I've never liked poetry. Every teacher I've ever had has brutalized it."

Joe replies, "I can teach poetry to anyone. It is the one thing I'm completely confident that I can do." I'm a believer. You would be, too.

The next poem is "Incident" by Countee Cullen. A volunteer shares why this poem is her favorite, "It's just one thing to think about; I liked that." Another student says she likes the point of view.

Joe says, "Anyone want to touch on that more?"

Ashley hesitates, "Well, every kid has a childhood. It can shape that kid for life, just like this moment shaped the author."

Joe explains pathos, another two-minute teachable moment on literary devices. Joe uses every opportunity for teaching. He is aware that weaving these terms into daily discussion will improve their relevance and help students begin to use them to describe literature. These constant connections to larger themes help students connect literature across genres and time. I wish someone had done this for me in high school. My English classes were filled with quizzes and vocabulary.

When the students begin the discussion of the poem's weaknesses, the first one explains that the poem is one-dimensional, has only one point and no deeper layers. I expect Joe to argue with her. I saw more than a surface meaning in the work.

Joe says, "And that's a weakness?" forcing the student to think through her own evaluation, instead of offering his. This is impressive. I know too many teachers who relish giving answers. I'm one of them.

Since teenagers will tell me I'm wrong about everything, it's nice to show off once in awhile. Not Joe. He knows that leading a student to her own answer pays off in further study of literature more than a simple answer ever could.

When she finishes her evaluation of the poem, he says, "Anyone agree or disagree with what was said?"

Laurel says, "Yes! It *is* one-dimensional, but that's a strength."

Joe smiles. "What would Hemingway think about it? How about Hawthorne?" Suddenly the conversation takes an analytical turn. The students are forced to see through the lens of style. Hemingway is a different writer from Hawthorne. Hemingway's work is often composed of simple, clipped sentences that move quickly from one scene to the next. Hawthorne's words dance together in an intricate waltz, one illuminating the next. It is intimidating, difficult text. Joe has asked which author's work is more closely linked to the style of this poem. This is precisely what American Literature students should be able to do: know a wide variety of works well enough to discuss and compare them as they gain understanding throughout the year. These students can. That didn't happen from a textbook; it took a skillful teacher to push their understanding to this level.

The students begin looking at the use of black and white imagery in the next poem, again driven by a student's response to it. Joe comments, "Poets look at the minute to talk about the infinite. This one made me think of Thoreau . . . to die and never have lived." Students nod in agreement. I love it. Not a single student says, "Who's Thoreau?"

He continues, "Have you seen this going on in *Native Son*? How? Where? Are there subtle images?"

Several students reach in their bags for their novels. Joe has kept these students reading nightly throughout the year. He designs projects that are innovative and fun, but they always lead back to a greater understanding of the novel being read. *Native Son* is a black man's powerful narrative of growing up in America. It is a perfect complement to the Harlem Renaissance poems of the Poetry Sweet Sixteen. One enriches the understanding of the other.

Michelle says, "Everything is white." Several students jump in with white images from the novel.

Joe responds, "Yes, remember it is even snowing." A few students break into surprised smiles. I am sure most students miss symbolism in the novels they read; but they delight in its discovery. It is like the fortune inside the cookie: the unexpected treat. A careful teacher pulls these images together for students and helps them see the meaning behind the text, hoping that perhaps in the next novel, the students might see them on their own.

Michelle says, "I didn't get it before, but now that we're talking about it, it makes sense." Others nod, flipping through the pages before them.

Joe continues, "Think back to the Puritans." Most American Literature courses begin there. In our school students read *The Crucible* to help them see this time period. Sharp teachers know to spiral curriculum, to revisit concepts, ideas, and themes presented earlier so that students continue to hear the echoes as they add more knowledge. Joe has woven this background together in a notable way. He says to his class, "There were three concepts the Puritans left us with; does anyone remember what they were? I'll be really impressed if you can recall these." You've got to figure each one of these students wants to impress him.

"Simplicity," Taylor calls out.

"Yes, and . . . ," Joe waits. He gives her a bright grin.

Ashley says, "Grace, and spirituality?" her voice hesitating, unsure.

Joe nods, "Yes, spirituality or *God*—a divine mission. I'm impressed," their eyes meet. Ashley blushes, pleased. "Americans still value simplicity. We like to say it quickly, just like the author does in this poem." The students are thinking.

We all are, watching Joe.

I shudder to say this. If I had to bet money on it, I'd say Joe probably won't be teaching at Kennett much longer. Here's why. When students first arrived this morning, a few asked if Joe had found his CDs. He said no, they were still missing. He told me he came in to school the day before and all of his CDs were gone from his desk drawer. Teachers can feel like they're under constant assault as pens, staplers, and coins disappear frequently from their rooms. I know the students I watched that morning wouldn't take anything from Joe. There is mutual respect and authentic fondness between them, but Joe's room is used by others when he is on his prep period. Those students don't know Joe. Trading rooms is in itself a major inconvenience, but every teacher in our building lives with it because we have grown out of our current facility and can't get the townspeople to agree on a solution. Teachers have to quickly grab the supplies they need to correct student work or make parent phone calls, plan units, and so on, then get out of their rooms when classes change, so another teacher can take over the space. If you forget something it means interrupting a class to retrieve it. The days are gone when students could call A-20 Mr. Fernald's room because it is also study hall one hour and some other teacher's room in the afternoon. It seems like a good solution for the use of space, but it is wearing on a teacher. Teachers want order. They want to display work and guarantee it will be respected by others. They can control that when the space is theirs. When sharing rooms begins, discouragements mount. One teacher who left last spring for a teaching job in a beautiful new building said to me, "I just want my own classroom." It's a pity I couldn't give it to her.

Joe contemplated leaving last year. He found a district that offered him more money. He struggled with his wish to stay with the students from our valley, and his need to be respected as a professional. One sign of that respect is, of course, salary. Our starting salary is $23,216.00. After taxes our newest teachers take home about $300.00 every week. I don't care how many lives you change in a year; if you can't plan to buy a house eventually or dig out of the debt from college loans, you'll consider other work that can make that happen. And yes, I know our local taxpayers are overburdened and unwilling to change this, but someone has to. I will bet that Joe will move into an administrative position or to another district to improve his salary within the next few years. What a loss for students. Joe loves teaching, but don't you think eight years after he left college he should at least have crested the $40,000.00 mark? If we want teachers to stay, we'll have to pay them what they're worth. It seems that too many good teachers leave the classroom because they can't advance much as teachers. We ought to change that. Joe is a master teacher; think of how much he would be worth to your child's education.

I feel fortunate to observe the many accomplished teachers at Kennett. I leave their classrooms inspired to redesign my own. I watch their students, alive with curiosity, and return to my own room working harder. But observing my peers is part of my job. My colleagues work in isolation almost all of the time. Teachers rarely observe each other; it isn't an expectation here in America. We could learn from the Japanese where teachers plan in teams, perfecting a model lesson, then trying it out in front of their team. They revise together and try again. It's a method clearly defined in *The Teaching Gap,* and our English teachers would love to try it, but it takes money. Release time for teachers is expensive; budgets are bust. It is a missed opportunity to make all teachers better. It would also make the job less isolating, a factor cited by many as a reason they left teaching. It would mimic the surgical classrooms where medical students observe a master surgeon at work. It is good professional practice.

If I can make it happen, my children will one day have American Literature with Joe Fernald. He's demanding, and students leave thinking more critically. They leave listening to each other and reasoning with an attention to textual evidence that makes their arguments credible. They leave confident they can discover the meanings layered within a novel on their own. Joe will probably never win Teacher of the Year or be recognized for his numerous talents with cash, but he reminds me that sometimes the best and brightest students still choose education. They could do anything and be successful, but they choose to give their lives to teenagers, and we are all better for it.

painting

*We can't give children rich lives, but we can give them the lens to
appreciate the richness that is already there in their lives.*

—Lucy Calkins

I almost missed it.

In the rush to complete and bind second-quarter portfolios and
compute grades, I almost missed one of those gifts that keeps me in
teaching, just when I needed it most. A stack of essays stood waiting
on my desk all weekend and I avoided seeing them. I laid the Sunday
newspaper across them, baked peanut butter cookies right beside
them, but I didn't read them. I knew each one would take a slow and
careful reading plus a patient crafting of my response, and I was exhausted. The below-zero temperatures had set in and they had si-
phoned off the last bit of energy I had. I'm a native Oregonian and will
never adjust to the full blast of winter here in New England.

My spirits were sagging that weekend as well. The school board had
voted to not retain the inspiring, hardworking principal in our building
and wouldn't reveal their reasons. The stack of student work was a re-
minder of the 5:15 wake-up call that awaited on Monday. I feared these
final products. These essays would show what they understood about
our latest genre study on memoir, but they might also force me to face
my many failures in teaching this year . . . the students who still abandoned every book they started or couldn't demonstrate the concept of
revision, or the ones who still asked what a rubric is after spending two
quarters in my room. Sometimes it seems easier to dwell on those students instead of the ones who are spreading their wings in writing.

I made a large cup of hazelnut coffee and settled onto my couch by the window. I happened to pick up Catherine's piece first. Catherine is a sensitive student and a committed writer, but up to this point her work had been centered too often on fiction filled with flowery romances and heartbreak. She was beginning to break out of that in short pieces she had shared with the class, but it wasn't until I began reading her piece of memoir that I began to see the writer. She captured the conversation she had had with her Grandfather Pepe, as he lay dying. She showed us the fears of a nine-year-old girl forced to say good-bye to a grandparent she adores. This was a well-crafted piece, yet she had told me when she turned it in that she wasn't satisfied with it yet. I could sense this was a turning point for her. Learning to develop a piece of writing, then facing the questions that nag you on subsequent readings is one mark, in my mind, of a writer.

I glanced at the next, Eddy's triumphant story of nailing his seventh-grade science teacher with a water balloon on the last day of school, and smiled. The playful approach to his topic and the self-awareness of a boy feeling all-powerful with a simple pint of water resulted in a strong piece worthy of a second and third reading. He had shared the beginning of this in author's chair, which had inspired many of my writers. Eddy is a storyteller and this genre study honored that. He told this with a flourish of detail from the battlefield of the classroom to the moment outside, but it was more than just a story. Eddy had written quite a few drafts. He had read his work to several students and asked for ideas. He was finally using the writing process because he had discovered a topic he cared enough about.

Cam is a talented and funny writer. His keen sense of observation brought just the right touch to his pieces and always brought the class to giggles. He had completed several columns for our team newspaper on local oddities, but the memoir piece was truly inspired. As I sat on my couch that day I found a final draft that explored the topic in far greater depth than his first draft had. This was victory in itself. I find that natural writers often think one draft is good enough and refuse to rework and rethink. Cam took me on a tour of the Recess Football League from his sixth-grade year at Madison Elementary School. He captured the essence of memoir with this line, "I could hit the rewind button on the remote control of life and see it frame by frame." From his view as an eighth grader, the days with multiple recesses looked ideal. His look back helped all of my students remember carefree days before the stress and social demands of middle school took over.

I noticed how Cam's football piece played with time, one of the key freedoms of this genre. As Randy Bomer (1995, 165) says, "A writer may begin at the present and skip to the past, allowing the reader to see how the present is old and heavy with history, how the writer is this person today as a result of what happened to him then."

I went on to read Billy's tribute to a favorite teacher who had recently died. He used several snapshots from his days in her third grade to show her compassion. This piece was organized efficiently and told with an attention to detail I hadn't seen before. I knew it was evidence of the strong connection that exists between reading and writing. Billy has already read thirty books this school year and the change that has made in his writing is remarkable. I could celebrate the child willing to say how much he loved his teacher, as well as his passion for reading that had brought such a maturity to his writing. By now, I didn't need coffee to keep me on task.

It struck me that this genre study resulted in the best writing of the year from not only a few students, but many. I believe it is particularly well-suited for this tumultuous age. Eighth graders are caught between childhood and adulthood. They cling to cartoons and toys they bring to class, gel pens and notes, grudges and Disney videos. Yet they reach for adulthood, grappling with tough issues like depression, eating disorders, sexual relationships, and suicide. They are growing up too fast and anxious to grow up faster. I found my students not only willing to look back at their lives and try to find meaning in the memories they held, but inspired to craft moving tributes to their past.

My own teaching has been invigorated this year by the work of Randy Bomer, as described in his book *Time for Meaning: Crafting Literate Lives in Middle and High School.* In the past I have presented models of writing and encouraged individual goals, organized portfolios and developed a workshop classroom that helped students discover their strengths and build on them. I allowed students choice over topic and genre. If following a passion, I let a student write many pieces of fiction or poetry, ignoring other genres for months. I encouraged diversity, but I didn't require it. I reached many and missed others with this approach.

This year we study the elements of a genre through strong models presented over a four-week period and they attempt a piece of writing in that genre at the same time. I encourage imitation of structure. I ask students to work out of their comfort zones and write what they think they cannot. And I practice what I preach. A turning point in our genre study came the day I shared my own piece, "Ashes." It tells of my struggles, as an insecure seventh grader, trying to deal with my father's alcoholism. I discussed the ways I could have approached the piece and the many drafts I had written and shared with my own writing group of teachers that meets weekly after school. I listened to their comments and wrote them on my draft, just as I ask them to do in author's chair. Genre studies have inspired my writing and transformed my classroom.

And then I read Dan's piece. Dan is one of those quiet students who will place himself in the back of a class. He completes his work dutifully. He is cooperative, but rarely volunteers an opinion. He writes well, but does most of his work outside of class and rarely shows his work to others. He had struggled with this genre. Each day I presented a model and we brainstormed elements of memoir writing onto a large piece of chart paper that hung in the front of the class. We discussed "the making of things from the chaos of experience" (Bomer 1995, 159). Each day Dan sat with his empty journal when we began our silent writing time and did not find a topic.

Dan is in my advisory group and had mentioned a week earlier that the holidays were kind of melancholy for him this year because of the long absence of his father. I finally sat down next to him one day in writing workshop and asked him if he would consider writing about the last time he had seen his father. He said, "No. Nothing happened. I didn't know it was going to be the last time."

I said, "I know. But now you do. Memoir is often about looking back on something that has happened through new eyes. It might be worth a try."

He wrote little that day. I felt nervous about pushing him, but felt he had the maturity to approach a difficult topic and make it his own. I saw only a paragraph of his efforts later that week and it didn't seem to be going anywhere. As I sat on my couch watching a bitter wind whip across the front lawn, I picked up Dan's essay entitled "Painting" with a sigh. I was sure Dan had chosen something safe like learning to paint in kindergarten. Instead, I got this:

If my life were a painting, my dad would be fading off more and more. Even though I darken the lines that make him over and over he just fades off. It's getting to the point where I'm starting to know less and less of what colors he is and what shapes he consists of. Sure I have dropped the brush too, and I'm not putting the blame on anyone, but the more tears I cry for him the more his picture drops off the page. I see less and less of him, and off my painting he fades more and more.

Where the red paint splashes is when he went to jail. He has been in jail now for a little over two years. It's really hard to have red paint splashed over my painting but even harder that he is fading off altogether.

The last week I was with him was before I noticed he was diminishing off my painting. He was diminishing, but I didn't notice it. I was more focused on the unstraight lines and dark colors. I visited him at his parents where he was staying. Conversations of plans for the future had started to make my picture very sketchy. I went for lots of walks with him. One I remember most vividly was walking down a railroad track talking about stupid things I don't remember, but weren't very significant. He said he wanted to show me something, but wouldn't tell me what. It was a surprise. It was a tunnel. An old abandoned tunnel used for something a long time ago. Him going to jail was never discussed though, even though I knew it was a possibility. I never would let myself believe that it might really happen. Him going to jail was never a reality in my mind. My father's slight arrogance slid him from believing that also, or admitting to me, or informing me of what was going on. Spending time with him and his family I saw a lot of blues, and grays. Silent dinners, and long walks painted these colors. Lots of secrets were involved in that visit. I knew he was into drugs, but he never said it. Soon the shapes on my painting had started to change from scurvy, unruly lines to being sharp, and drawn with anger and confusion.

Also while I was there, we rode four-wheelers through corn crops in Amish country. They grow their corn in strips so there were patches of land free of crops to ride on. We got nowhere, just like our conversations. Then even though it was too big for me at the time to control he let me drive it. Let me take over. He sat back and let me do the driving for awhile. I streamed through the grass with him behind me, yelling instructions over the sound of the motor to me, helping me keep it under control. He even grabbed the handlebars a few times. I wondered what I'd do if he wasn't there. If he wasn't there at all.

Saying good-bye, little did I know was spilling some of my paint. He and I both cried as we usually do when we say good-bye because we both know it's good-bye for a long period of time. He knew, maybe not that well, but he knew it would be for a lot longer this time, causing extra sorrow. His good-bye was more sincere this time, and more emotional. Blacks, and dark reds filled my painting real thick.

Now I still miss him and try my hardest to keep drawing him in carefully, but I'm starting to run out of paint. I will see him again soon and I hope he has some to fill my almost empty bucket.

His work unfolded like a marvelous surprise. This was an achievement. I rushed to read it to my husband, who's an engineer. He puts up with my enthusiasm for adolescent writing, but rarely shares it. He listened, but not just politely. He took it from my hands and read it again. The next day I shared it with my principal, who had tears in her eyes after the first paragraph and asked for a copy so she could write a personal note to the author. The secretary stopped typing to listen. Dan has agreed to let me share it with my classes and I look forward to the opportunity to show them another strong memoir model.

Today brought one of the gifts of a New Hampshire winter: an early release from school due to a powerful Nor'easter snowstorm. I brought home another stack of memoirs to read and I'm eager to get to them.

when our lives teach

*Writing is work, and it can leave you gray with exhaustion,
can devour your days, can break your heart.*

—Scott Russell Sanders

I was lucky one year to have a group of ninth graders for English, many of whom had also been in my eighth-grade writing workshop the year before. I knew these kids. I knew their parents. We shared stories at the start of class each day, a quick chat to help us connect to the new students who had joined us from surrounding towns, and to process this transformation to high school. Our relationship started strong and only increased as the semester wore on, as Jason and Torin brought their guitars to our Coffee House Poetry event on Fridays, as Kelli read her witty journal entries and Laurel told us stories of her sisters, as Jenna finally got her belly ring. I stood back amazed at the physical and emotional changes each was making as they morphed into young adults. It was destined to be an exceptional teaching experience and I eagerly planned for our time together.

This changed one weekend when I was devastated by a tragedy. Our close friend David lost his daughter Anna in a horrific collision on a dark stretch of highway in Illinois. Anna had been my children's babysitter and was much beloved by our entire family. We had been close when we lived in Michigan, so this wasn't a tragedy that anyone in my school had heard of or could understand. I felt very alone in my grief and afraid that my students would trivialize her death: just another drunk driving casualty. I didn't feel able to teach. I didn't feel able to scramble eggs. I was afraid to share this personal pain with my students and wished I could retreat behind my desk, become the kind of teacher I wasn't: disconnected, uninterested, content-centered. Perhaps then I could pretend it hadn't happened for at least a few hours each day.

I shared Anna's death briefly in our morning chat, more as a warning than anything else. They understood. They cut a wide path around me that day and worked quietly. I told them I would be gone from school while we traveled back for the funeral. They were kind, but they couldn't know the depth of what I felt and I had no desire for them to. Their lives had been free of this kind of tragedy and I was thankful for that, even as I watched them quickly move to the next important topic: the Dave Matthews concert in Boston.

Following the funeral I looked at my plans for a unit on persuasive writing. I always plan to write with my classes now: I use my drafting and revisions as a model for students of the process of creating writing. Students need more than exemplary models of writing; they need to see how those pieces are crafted. I knew I wanted to tell the story I had just experienced, but was hesitant to risk the emotional toll writing about this loss would take. I wrestled with this decision over several days.

I remembered reading *Where the Red Fern Grows* to my first group of students, third graders, and feeling so awkward when the tears started. I thought being in the teaching role would somehow insulate me from fully feeling the story as I had the first time I'd read it, but instead I was as moved as ever. I believe students want to connect to us in sorrow as well as in joy, but I had no wish to parade my current emotions in front of teenagers. This was not fiction: I was raw. It was more than I could bear some days. Would I be able to write this piece with my class? It was an opportunity to teach them about drinking and driving, compassion and writing. It was an extended teachable moment: that rare time when learning is natural and lasting. But it was a risk.

I began with a draft, a beginning I bled into my keyboard one evening when my students were still considering topics. I brought the piece in and explained that I knew my topic, but was struggling with how to tell Anna's story. They read silently, respectfully. My students were gentle editors of my work, unwilling to suggest any changes at all. Throughout the semester we had been moving between the roles of writers and editors, teachers and students. Those lines were not clear. I explained that I wanted to tell the world about Anna, to see my essay printed in our local paper at least, so it had to be good. I appreciated their supportive comments, but I needed editing.

It was the only invitation they needed. Several jumped in. The first suggestion came from Jason. He said, "You need to cut out all of this memory stuff while you're driving to the funeral. It just isn't that interesting." Ouch. Those memories were important to me, I explained. I was trying to show Anna, and it put my grief into words. I could wrap my arms around my pain by naming it. But I could also see his point. They were taking the reader away from my topic. I agreed to cut many of the memories in order to maintain momentum in the piece. I modeled deleting large portions of text to improve the focus of a piece of my own writing. It was good editing, but it also helped me understand what I am asking of my students when I suggest that they have wandered off topic and should cut sections of their work. It wasn't easy. When I brought in draft two the next day, Jason was gratified to see that I had used his suggestion. I respected his understanding of writing, a powerful message to give a young writer. And truthfully, it improved the piece.

I learned my own lessons that month. I replayed moments in my mind and tried to make the words work on paper, but I was too immersed in how this experience had shattered my world to understand the impatience of another reader. Only other readers could provide me with perspective when I was tied emotionally to my writing. I thought about the number of wrenching pieces I had read over the years and how badly my students needed editors like they were being for me. Did I provide enough time for them to work through their writing with others? No. Too often they finished their work alone so we could move on to another piece. This rush left the process incomplete. I needed to have them linger longer over less. One piece reworked many times is worth more in the development of a writer than several first drafts cleaned up for a grade.

My writing mini-lessons sprang from my struggles with this piece. One day we worked through possible alternatives for the verb *crushed,* a word I felt communicated the quick demolition of three lives. We practiced reading one sentence with a period, then with a semicolon, which they preferred, once they understood its use. I used a simple exercise that I use often with a class to force them to discriminate: underline your favorite line. Underline the line that leaves you wondering. Underline the line that hooks you and makes you keep reading. If an important line is balanced, sometimes the entire sentence lands hard on the last few words. Consider this one:

> A sad tale, grieving families, and sense of dismay that twenty-five-year-old Brandon could take the lives of three so swiftly, leaving the scene with broken ankles and shame, but breath in his lungs.

These were lessons I couldn't teach using someone else's writing. I knew the choices I was making as I wrote and I could make my thinking transparent for my students. One lesson was reinforced often throughout the unit: writers make choices about what to include in a piece based on how it will impact the reader's understanding of the story. I'm not sure my fourteen- and fifteen-year-old students had ever really considered that before.

One dramatic revision lesson came by accident, really. I had emailed my piece to a friend who is also a terrific writer. At this point we had been working on my piece in class for a few days. My friend said I needed to cut the piece in half if I expected it to be published. My students balked. We would lose the story, they felt. I agreed with them, but this man had published twenty-five books, so I figured his instincts were sharp. I asked them to work with a partner to make huge cuts, while trying to maintain the flow of the story, and then we would compare the results together. The conversations that occurred showed a strong understanding of structure and organization. Not surprisingly, each pair cut many of the same sections. It was clear that these were less necessary. For me, this revision was brutal, but my students learned something important. They are often unwilling to cut out what they have crafted. It feels like wasted work in a world where filling the page has been the goal more than telling the story well. Our students have been programmed to complete the worksheet, complete journal entries of half a page or paragraphs with ten sentences. Is it any wonder they shudder at the thought of cutting lines? If you are writing to fill a requirement, the labor of sentences, one stacked upon another, cannot be undone. If you are writing to send a message, whole drafts can fill the recycling bin. I'm not sure this one model can alter what they've experienced for the last ten years in school, but more experiences like this one could. Our writing workshops have to allow for the work of real writers. Days of writing can end up cut from the piece. Revision takes time. It looks unproductive. It is imprecise.

I kept writing about the funeral. It was a fitting tribute to Anna, and I was thankful for that. We had joined a line of more than one hundred cars that wound through the streets of Livonia toward the cemetery. Many people sat waiting at intersections for a very long time, following our cars with their eyes, respectful, not impatient. A lone policeman stood in the wind, waving us through each blinking intersection. I wanted to get out and explain to the drivers of all those minivans. It didn't seem right that soccer players were still going to play their games and parents would cheer at them. The world needed to stop and take notice. Anna was gone. However, when it came to the writing, most of this experience had to go. My focus was more on persuading people to think about drunk driving, not the funeral of this wonderful girl. As I discussed this with students, we looked at the choices that were dictated by audience. I could tell the story of Anna for the youth group or friends that had known her like we did, including the details of a funeral they had shared. For the general public, I must tell the same story differently. It is an important lesson about writing said succinctly by my friend Roy Peter Clark: tools not rules. Teach students that writers make decisions about their writing for the audience and the purpose of the piece. What works in one may not work in another. Writers use tools to craft a piece, not rules to contain it.

I talked to my students about the need to write balanced editorials. This meant I had to try to understand the drunk driver's position in this tragedy. Every person has a story. I didn't know Brandon's, but I was pretty sure he wasn't happy to have caused so much misery. I didn't want to see his side; in fact, I avoided it. When I finally wrote the paragraph, my students hated it. They said I was far too easy on him. It opened up a lesson on mistakes, forgiveness, and empathy. As difficult as it was to put myself in Brandon's shoes, I was sure he was now on a difficult road himself. I discussed the possible sentencing options that he faced: anything from probation to twenty-four years in jail. He has a child that will grow up without him. The paragraph stayed in because I wanted it there. My students never agreed with me, but this was another lesson: in the end, the writer decides.

An unexpected bonus had developed over these weeks: because this was a real story from my life, I had the full attention of my students. I can't imagine they would have been as committed to multiple readings of a story from an author they didn't know. Yet they also watched those multiple readings improve the piece. They saw the craft of writing in practice, the slow and steady work it takes, the value of peer discussion and compromise. They wanted my essay published. We were writing for a real purpose. We learned together how to take emotions and turn them into persuasive writing. Instead of preaching revision, I lived it.

The piece appeared in our local paper the weekend before senior prom. It provoked a strong reaction among friends and fellow teachers, all pleased that I had tackled a difficult issue at a time when people needed to hear it. I'm sure it made others uncomfortable, even angry. One fellow teacher approached me in the cafeteria to talk about the editorial. He shared the loss of his own daughter to alcohol. I had worked beside this man for five years and had never heard this most important story of his life. Writing forces connections.

David, Anna's father, sent my editorial to the judge deciding on Brandon's sentence. He sent it with the victim impact statements he and his younger daughter Megan wrote. Brandon Hurst was sentenced to ten years in prison for the deaths of Anna and her college friends, Chris and Sally. He cried at the sentencing and begged forgiveness from the families. The sentencing happened in August, so I wasn't able to share it with my class. I wasn't surprised, however, when one of my former students approached me during the first week of school and asked me the result of his sentencing. Students don't forget the power of an experience like this one. Hopefully, they'll remember the lessons about writing as well.

I couldn't repeat this experience. I can't pass out "One for the Road" when my next class studies persuasive writing and expect for it to have the same impact. It changed classroom life because I was learning along with my students. That I can repeat: in fact, I'm writing a first-draft response this weekend to *The Crucible* which I'll use with my American Literature students next week. It will undoubtedly be altered by the twenty-nine students that fill the seats in my stuffy, portable classroom. Hopefully it will expand their understanding of the writing process as well.

Anna was an artist, a poet, a singer, an actress. What a tribute to her life if through her story I have helped my students learn the craft of writing, so that they can create art from their own lives.

one for the road

A familiar story stole into our house on March 17th. A drunk driver named Brandon sped to the wrong side of an Illinois highway, directly into the path of five college sophomores who were going to volunteer at an elementary school for spring vacation week. Their car was crushed and in a fraction of a second, three students died. Anna, the eldest daughter of our close friend, was one of them. We heard the shattered voice of her father that afternoon and our hearts were broken.

We may pretend we are prepared for a moment like this, but we aren't. It felt like a story we have scanned in our newspapers too often. The innocent victims, seatbelts fastened, and a driver alert and sober round a corner on a fast-moving interstate in the black of night and are instantly crushed. The skid marks were 8 feet long; they barely saw him.

Reduced to these simple facts, you can keep reading. You know there is more to the story, but similar reports have been repeated so many times now, you can almost sense the particulars. A sad tale, grieving families, and sense of dismay that twenty-five-year-old Brandon could take the lives of three so swiftly, leaving the scene with broken ankles and shame, but breath in his lungs.

But you didn't know Anna.

Anna was our children's baby-sitter, a beautiful wonder who was filled with joy. Anna called herself solar-powered and raked leaves just to jump in them. It made me smile just to be near her. She was deeply spiritual and more at peace than any girl I've ever known. I remember we came home one night to find her fallen asleep on the couch with a pink fairy wand still in her hand. She was the baby-sitter who played.

She dressed up with my daughter; she assembled Legos with my son. She made cookies and cleaned her dishes. She picked daisies from the field behind the house and made an elaborate chain that lay wilted on my daughter's nightstand for weeks.

One summer we went camping. It started pouring down rain just after we'd set up our tents, and while we huddled in ours, Anna burst out into the clearing with two friends and danced barefoot in the rain, her face turned up toward the sky, smiling delightedly. I peered out the tent flap and envied her; she was so free.

Anna sang the prayers in church on many Sundays. Her voice had a luminous quality that hung in the air a moment longer than expected. We sang those prayers at her funeral and the tears poured down my face, my tissue a sodden mass in my hand, as I listened for Anna. I could almost hear her. My daughter patted my leg and said, "Mom, it's okay," but it wasn't. It won't be.

Anna will not celebrate her twentieth birthday this year because Brandon went out with friends to drink at Marley's bar in honor of St. Patrick's Day. Who served them pitcher after pitcher? Who watched them leave with car keys in hand? Who looked away and shrugged, *Those guys shouldn't be driving?* Walk into any bar in the valley this weekend and you might see bloodshot eyes and a sloppy sway, the obvious signs of someone who is wasted. But you won't ask how that drunk will get home tonight.

We all look the other way.

Brandon stepped into his new Ford Taurus not intending to kill anyone. He is a husband and a father. He might cringe at the word *murderer*. His friends drove him from the bar to get his car. I bet they'll say he seemed okay and if he'd said anything at all they'd have driven him home. That's what friends are for.

We traveled from our house in Kearsarge to the funeral services in Livonia, Michigan, across a barren pre-spring landscape that was appropriately bleak. In a sanctuary that seated 550 we squeezed together to make room for Anna's high school drama friends, her aunts and uncles and weeping grandparents, her stunned college friends, and still others who filled the folding chairs in the waiting room beyond. I held Anna's little sister Megan in my arms, a shell of the girl I knew last August.

For the last four years I have taught hundreds of teenagers English at Kennett Jr./Sr. High School. I've met wonderful young people with bright futures, yet I see the arrests in the paper each week. There are drunk drivers on our roads, the same roads that carry our athletes, our musicians, our neighbors and friends.

It could happen in Conway. It could happen to someone you know. Will you drive him to his car? Will you watch him walk before you and think, *He shouldn't be driving?* Will you look the other way as he takes off toward another road and toward another child?

Will you?

about more than baseball

For better or worse each child has an aspiration, a deep longing to become something greater than he or she is at the moment.

—Donald Graves

When the first batter steps up to the plate, the silence that surrounds the field is painful. It only lasts a few seconds, since it betrays the anxiety we are trying so hard to hide from the boys. There is scattered applause, a self-conscious, "Let's go Green," and Jimmy sends the first pitch flying toward the plate. Strike one. Cheers. Laughter. People gather against the fence.

"I guess there'll be no sitting for this one," a mother offers as she joins the others.

The extra innings began at 5:00, the game suspended by darkness the night before when the teams remained tied at the end of the tenth inning. The winner of this game tonight would advance to the finals. The Green team had won the championship seven years in a row and had a 14-1 record this summer. Their opponents, the Reds, were responsible for that one stunning loss the Greens had suffered the week before. A fluke, they thought. No one expected this close game. The Reds could taste the promise of an underdog victory. The Greens simply had to win, everyone expected them to.

My son came to watch his good friend Matt. Matt approached before the game, sweat already forming across his upper lip as he paced with his new bat and freshly washed green uniform. He is a natural talent and a dedicated player, forgoing all other sports to concentrate on baseball. The rumor has it his father was once such a promising player, but his dreams were cut short with an injury. Matt is now the promise. Tonight he is nervous.

The Green pitcher throws two more strikes and knocks out the first Red player quickly. The second batter makes it to first base. Jimmy is the pitcher, a student I had a year ago in eighth grade. He is quiet and gentle, a large kid with fine, blond hair. He is all kindness, always polite, never a bad word for anyone. He is a gift to a classroom and I adore him. He has a talented, athletic older brother and a family history of athletic success. I can feel the pressure on him. I want him to do well tonight; I watch him eye his coach as he surveys the next player before him.

It is Torin. I love this kid. A student of mine for the last two years, Torin has grown from an awkward adolescent into a considerate and sensitive young man this year. He shared his excitement with me in the spring when he was chosen captain of this Red Babe Ruth team. I know what baseball means to him. How can I choose a side in this game? They are all my kids.

Torin wrote a memoir for my class about playing in a baseball tournament three years before. It was his best piece of writing yet, with the tension building as the story reached the last inning, the last fly ball heading toward his glove. Only he dropped it. He had felt the loss of the entire game in his hands and it had taken him three years to write that story. Here he stands again, with the weight of their season on his slight shoulders.

He stands tall and surveys the crowd and the field. I imagine he's writing his next story, smelling the leather in the glove poised inches behind him, feeling the sun melt his polyester shirt to his tanned back. He practices a strong swing and steps into the batter box. *Come on, Torin,* I plead silently. I'm a traitor standing here with these Green parents, hoping this Red batter will blast the ball with all he has.

He does. It is an impressive hit, above the head of the center fielder. Matt races to catch the bounce off the back boundary and quickly sends the ball to second base, holding Torin at first. Cheers on all sides. I watch Torin give a thumbs-up to his teammate on second and smile.

My son turns to see if I noticed Matt's great play. "Yes," I nod, "Impressive."

The Reds manage to score soon after and put another man on base. There are errors by the Green team in the infield, balls mishandled, nerves straining these kids to the breaking point. Torin is now on third base and with a quick infield hit, the bases are loaded. Matt's mom lights up a cigarette and paces just behind the fence.

"Jesus," she says.

Walking up to the plate is a slightly built kid, his face shadowed by the helmet. I know the walk, I think, but I can't see.

"Who is that?" I ask a father nearby.

"Ethan Davis."

My heart sinks. Ethan with the bases loaded. No wonder his chest is thrust out before him as if to ward off the weight of this. He has too much to lose. He appears confident, ready. I search the crowd for his grandparents. I hope they are here. Ethan was a quiet, reluctant student when I first met him. We began to connect when he worked on a piece tracing his personal history. He struggled to tell the story of separating from his parents and moving here to live with his grandparents. He had tried his dad's house, then his mom's, then his dad's again. It was complicated and he was a struggling writer. One day he came back at lunch for another conference and said, "Mrs. Kittle, I have to get this right." It wasn't about the writing.

When he arrived in the valley, he had joined every sports team he could, often riding his bicycle several miles to practice. He was a strong competitor; he never gave up. He had earned the respect of his teammates and cherished it. His final portfolio contained several short pieces about important games, but the piece we had first worked on together remained his favorite. Probably because he had gotten it right; the story made sense. The reader understood why he had to move. I believe Ethan finally did as well.

He swings at the first pitch and misses. Yikes. I can't watch. I have to.

The pitcher eyes his father, who gives him a thumbs-up, "Another one just like that, Jimmy," he says.

Two balls, one strike. Ethan swings hard at the next and pops it up near the foul line, right in front of the plate. He waits to run, then starts forward, as the catcher and pitcher move in to catch it.

"Call it!" the coach yells. There is just a hint of desperation in his croaky voice.

The boys answer, "Got it!" as the ball nicks the edge of the catcher's mitt and hits the dirt between them. The catcher scrambles to snag it and tag the plate as he sends the ball toward second. Double play. From riches to ruins in a few seconds, Ethan hangs his head as he walks toward the dugout. Damn.

In silence the teams change positions. The first Green batter is Eddy, a small twelve-year-old, half the size of some of his teammates. He is the last batter in their line-up, but the team has to start where they left off the night before. His mother was diagnosed with breast cancer this fall. She is our school secretary, her two children attend our school, and her husband is a coach and study hall monitor. We have all agonized over the uncertainty. She told me she had asked Eddy to cut the grass one afternoon soon after she heard, but to leave the Indian paintbrush still growing in the back field. When she looked out later, he had cut a large heart around it. It was the only sign of what he was carrying.

He doesn't swing. He watches four pitches go by silently and takes his base as the crowd cheers.

I notice the pitcher and am relieved to not recognize him. They get the next batter out on a pop-up in the infield, but this pitcher is struggling. He is kicking the dirt, trying to gain ground as William approaches the plate. William has struggled to fit in at school. He is young and nice-looking, but exiled from almost everyone. I have never really understood why. He loves baseball and being a part of this team. They are winners. The count goes to 3-1, this pitcher still throwing far off the mark. William takes his base, as Jimmy heads to the plate, then curses in disgust. He throws the bat aside and jogs toward first. An intentional walk. I understand it is a smart strategy, but it feels unfair. Jimmy would have loved the chance to bring the runners in.

The bases are loaded. Matt steps forward. Cam cheers with the rest of the Green crowd. Matt not only pitches near 70 mph, he has a batting average that all the boys envy. He has struck out once in the last two seasons. Last week he hit a game-ending grand slam. The pitcher sends three balls across the plate. The count 3-0. Walking one in will tie this game, but a power hit would end it.

Strike one. Matt is surprised and steps away, then back quickly. He swings at the next, popping it up behind the backstop. The count now 3-2. The pitcher winds back and sends a beauty across the plate. I can't look. Unbelievably, it's a third strike, and Matt must face the crowd as he heads to the dugout. The Red crowd is jubilant, the Green silent. Matt's mom walks away from the fence; his father and sister cling helplessly to its wire frame, not moving. My son stares, unbelieving.

Two outs and the bases are loaded. This will be it. Kenny steps up. I'm grateful I barely know him, although I feel like I do, since one of my girls spent the entire year hopelessly in love with his every move. She wrote about him nightly in her journal, poetry and letters and dreams. His mother is seated near the fence, fraying the woven edges of her lawn chair. Kenny swings at the first, watches two balls go by, then swings and misses again. He steps away for a moment and looks at the dirt, the count 2-2. The next pitch is high, easy to read, and the count moves to 3-2. We all breathe silently. I just can't stand it. One pitch.

I want them all to win.

The pitch comes in and Kenny swings, catching the ball low and sending it over the pitcher's head as the runner races for home. Torin fields the ball to the second baseman, who tags the runner out. Over, in an instant.

I watch Torin approach the mound to keep from looking at the Green runners as they come in from the field. I'm happy to see the joy on Torin's face briefly before he is pulled into a subdued celebration. Green helmets rain from the dugout. My son is silent.

"Shit," says a mother near me.

It is a silent walk back to our truck past the flushed, tear-stained faces of kids I have known for years. I realize how lucky I am. If I had any other job, I might speed by this field on a summer's night with a quick glance at the players. Instead I know these boys; they have drawn me near with their stories and journals. This is my answer to the question I see in the papers regarding teaching: *Why would anyone want this thankless job?*

It is a privilege.

Weaving my life into the fabric of these adolescents is a gift indeed.

home run

Our lives are enriched by the doing. Never forget that.

—Tom Romano

That evening at the ball field I was writing the piece in my head as I watched the game. I was fully aware of details, moods, people, and conversations. I kept looking around, thinking, "This is a story." I didn't have a commitment from Heinemann; in fact, I hadn't even sent my work to an editor yet. I was just thinking like a writer, building on the work I had done in the teachers' writing group the year before. I knew that a realization of why I value teaching was coming to a head that evening. I wrote the piece as a tribute to summer, to teaching, and to this small town I live in. I really didn't have an audience in mind; I was writing for me.

I sent my draft to baseball fans I know. First, my father. Dad was once a fabulous pitcher. In fact, there's a newspaper clipping of him, poised in a windup with the headline, "Ostrem Pitches No-hitter Here." It captures my dad as a young man; it reminds me of what I missed in being born his daughter so many years later. My father was once in command of the field; how I would love to have seen that. In fact, the reason I cried at my first viewing of *Field of Dreams* was because I was suddenly sure of my greatest desire: I wanted to know my father before. Before he quit college, before the loss of my brother, before alcohol . . . when the world was full of promise and he was waiting to make his mark. My dad loved "about more than baseball," but he loves all my work just because it's mine.

I sent the piece to Don Graves and Don Murray because we share our work as writers through email. I knew they loved baseball and would enjoy the story. And there was this moment when I was wanting to show off a little, too. I liked that story. I'm always apprehensive once I hit "Send," though. My hand comes off the desk unconsciously as I seek to grasp the draft back from cyberspace. I'm never ready to share what I've written with such impressive, accomplished writers.

That afternoon Don Graves left a message on my machine to say I should check my email for thoughts from Murray. I know a piece is good when Don calls me, his delightful chuckle bursting into my kitchen. Don is full of energy and when he likes something, he pours out praise. Murray's read of the piece stunned me. He gave me a movie of his reading, including these words:

Christ another God damned Little League story with the parents making asses of themselves. A story that needs to be told but has been told many times, even by me.

I pictured him scowling at my draft, then rolling it up like a newspaper to smack me on the nose.

She's good. This moves right along. I am at the game. It looks easy, but it isn't. Strong narrative skills. She can write anything and carry the reader forward.

I want to hear more. My heart is starting to thump a little.

Hey, this isn't a story I've read. It's not a cliché parent story. It's not the cliché anti-sport piece, it is the story of a teacher who knows her kids and cares about them . . .

Yes, exactly. I feel understood. Thank you.

And I come to the end of the article and am knocked off my feet. . . . In Don Graves' terms, Penny has given me energy. I'm revived.

I sat at my desk reading and rereading his words. It was those daring words at the start that made his praise believable. Readers need to be honest to be credible. Teachers have to be honest. I was buoyed by the

Dons' support and started thinking about who else could read my story.

When school started again I saw Torin in the hall and rushed to congratulate him, since the win that night had sent the team on to the championship, where they won again. I told him I had been at the game and written a piece about it. I asked him if he was writing his own story of that day, and he said he'd thought about it. Yes! I pushed him over the next few weeks because I knew he was struggling with his sophomore coursework and, in particular, his English class. Literary analysis was not inspiring him; his grade was suffering. I wanted him to write for himself, for his own purpose, to remember the writing he was capable of, in hopes it would help him find a path through his class. I was also curious to hear his side of the intensity that night.

Over the course of the next few months I would mention his writing when I saw him, a simple, "Are you going to write that piece?" to remind him he had an eager audience awaiting his work. There were times when I wondered if this was fair; I wasn't doing this for scores of other kids I saw each day. I think what I've realized in the last few years is I have to seize the chances I find with students, wherever I find them. If I can push a kid a little further, then I ought to. Even if it means I can't do it for everyone.

One afternoon Torin stopped me in the lunch room with an envelope.

Mrs. Kittle,

This is the start of the story you've been asking for for some time. I finally got on it and here it is. Feel free to make all the changes you can, because there will be tons. Thanks.

Torin

These are the moments that keep me in teaching. He not only wrote the story, he invited me to help him improve it, although it had nothing to do with a grade. I eagerly opened the envelope and found three typed pages with all of the key events detailed. He took a journalistic stance and wrote like the writer I expect to see in the sports pages some day. He captured every moment, many I hadn't seen. If teachers can inspire their students to write for themselves, the game is over. We all win. I was dancing down the hall that day.

And wait, that was only the beginning, a quick sprint to first base. I sent Torin his piece back with comments and suggestions, encouraging him to finish the story and send it to me again. I also enclosed a copy of "about more than baseball" to show him what I had done. I told him it would be in my book and that the names would be changed, but he'd know who he was. This felt like an Atwell moment. You know how she mentioned her students passing drafts to each other secretly in the halls of their high school? I'd always wanted those students to be mine.

A few days later Torin's father called me. I'd met Doug the spring before, when he came to class to read from his favorite story, *Lake Wobegon*. I remember his hand trembling a little as he read, my students gathered politely, listening intently. He was the one parent who responded to my invitation and I appreciated it, however much it embarrassed Torin. Even in high school, parents should visit once in a while. Doug called to say he had read my piece and wanted me to know how much he enjoyed it. He said he was going to write his own version of that night, inspired by Torin and me. Suddenly it felt like I'd hit a double. Way cool. I could see that ball moving out of the infield.

And yet there's more . . .

Yesterday I was standing at the Xerox machine when a voice said, "This is for you." It was Torin's father, holding a plain, manila envelope. He told me he had been working on the piece and he would appreciate my comments and suggestions on his work. I told him he should comment on mine as well and send it back, since I always appreciate the suggestions of another reader. Teacher . . . child . . . parent: a miniwriting group. That's a rocket over the head of the outfielder. A triple, at least. I couldn't have predicted it. It was probably my most meaningful teaching moment of the year and it had nothing to do with school, really. That's something to think about.

Doug's piece was great. He knew a lot that I didn't that night; I saw the game a little differently from his view. Both Doug and Torin used baseball language that I don't know; their work had a different feel altogether. I'm scratching comments on Doug's piece this week, so I can return it to him. My own piece showed up in my mailbox this morning with Doug's remarks scribbled in the margins.

Consider what all of this activity has modeled for Torin. Writers share, write, and revise in company. We seek supportive feedback and criticism simply to make our writing better. We can span ages and purposes, perspectives and styles, but we share a love for language and the need to tell a story well. A baseball game might be seen in several ways, and those differing points of view will change the story. Any story. I'm sure Torin saw the love and support in his father's story, as I did. Torin will move from adolescence to adulthood and then away from home, but they'll always be able to look back at that game together, made more real by their writing. When I looked at our three pieces side by side, I saw the father who loves his son and watching him play well, the teacher who loves seeing her students achieve their dreams, and the young man who is devoted to the game.

That night last summer, Torin hit the home runs.

With our writing, we all have.

beyond courtship

I offer up my thanks to the fates of mate choice and can't believe my luck.

—Barbara Kingsolver

It was the Friday before Christmas vacation and I was straining to hold onto the attention of my ninth graders. They were scattered in pockets around the chairs forming a horseshoe before me, zippering backpacks to signal they were done with class for the day. I was reading *Of Mice and Men* to them, but their eyes kept wandering to the classroom door. It's a little annoying to see my students distracted, as if I'm not the most exciting thing in the room, but it isn't unusual and I've learned to get over it. I tried to keep reading, but noticed most weren't just glancing at the door, they were staring. I'd lost them. I put my finger in the page and leaned forward on my wooden stool to see what they were looking at.

Into the room stepped my husband, Pat. I barely registered the suit and tie, the large bouquet in his right hand, before he started singing an old Frankie Valli tune called "Can't Take My Eyes Off of You." My heart stopped. A deep flush started as I watched my students giddily glancing from him to me, enjoying this unexpected show. My husband was serenading me in front of my class!

I buried my face in my hands. Wow, he sings well. Please stop.

He was almost next to me in the front of the class, his voice, wavering just a little, the only sound in the room. My students had huge smiles; I couldn't believe he was talking about touching me, loving me, calling me baby in front of them.

I could die.

This was at once the most romantic thing that had happened to me in awhile and the most embarrassing. Every eye was on him. Students had stopped stuffing backpacks, half bent over their chairs, frozen in place.

It was our anniversary. I should've known. Pat has a way of thinking of original, wonderful things to do to honor our years together. It is one of many things I adore about him. And talk about courage; he was singing in front of a roomful of adolescents, the most severe critics I know. I began to breathe again as I thought he had come to the end of the song, but instead he slowly began the music that accompanies the chorus.

Do-do; do-do; do-do; do-do . . .

He rocked from side to side while my students joined in with rhythmic clapping. It was a whole-class performance . . . invigorating, and joyful. I was giggling now. I watched the smiling eyes of my students, remembering that this model of long-term love was missing in too many of their lives.

Pat had his arms outstretched, a nervous smile in his eyes, and he had clearly practiced for this moment. He was louder, more enthusiastic with each verse, and I was sinking into my stool. He continued steadily to the end of the chorus as my students cheered and applauded. I love it when my classroom explodes with this kind of spontaneous energy. Pat kissed me in front of them, gave me the flowers, and scooted out the door.

I was too self-conscious to move; I buried my face in the velvety touch of yellow roses. I couldn't exactly return to reading out loud. My cheeks burned.

"That was the coolest thing I've ever seen in my life," said Todd, the tough hockey player in the front row. Other students joined in laughing and commenting on Pat's willingness to make a fool of himself. I inhaled the roses and listened.

"Mrs. Kittle, how long have you been married?" Samantha asked.

"Sixteen years," I smiled.

"Geez. That's a long time. Congratulations on still, you know, liking each other," Samantha seemed lost in thought, her eyes peering from under long, red bangs to somewhere behind me.

"That's older than all of us," Todd added, snickering, "You're *old*, Mrs. Kittle."

"Not older than me," Kenn called out, reminding us, again, that it was his third time through this freshman course. We all laughed. The bell rang and we called out our have-a-nice-vacations as they hurried off to the halls.

I believe teaching, like marriage, is best when you make it past the courtship. My husband and I have a relationship that I value more each year we spend together. It has gone through innumerable changes in the almost twenty years we've been close, but those changes, like threads in a large quilt, create the story of who we are together. We are a powerful collaboration. As I often tell my students, I wish that everyone had the connection we share, one founded on honesty, support, and solid commitment. I wouldn't return to the first months of our relationship, just as I wouldn't return to my first year of teaching. They're both much better with age.

Because of our years together, Pat knows me better than anyone. He can tell much about my day by the way my bag hits the floor when I arrive home at night, by the way I hang my coat or greet our children. We walk our golden retriever Madison around our neighborhood each evening and talk, listening to the thoughts we share with no one else. We're rarely awkward with each other. There is routine and repetition, similar squabbles that try our patience, and shared moments we can recall with a word, a glance, a smile. It is nothing like the discovery that marks a new relationship. It is better.

Teaching, like love, begins with a kind of euphoria. These are my students, my classroom, my pencils and books. When you dream of becoming a teacher, seeing your name on the door and hearing the first few voices call out "Mrs. Kittle!" is immensely rewarding. There are many trials in even the first day, but the students rise to salute the flag and your eyes can settle on each one, absorbing the wonder and promise in their eyes, the gentleness that has been entrusted to you. It is a huge responsibility; it is terrifying.

Long ago Pat and I began with discovery. I remember the first kiss in his little green Toyota with the rain hammering the windshield and the smell of spring just outside the door. I remember the way my heart would pound when the phone rang at night. There was the dinner he cooked for us, our drive to the Oregon coast to hang glide, and the many questions I had. It seemed like I'd never uncover who he really was, but I wanted to try.

I remember reading Amanda's journal in my first teaching job in southern California. Her journal said I was her favorite teacher of all time and that she loved me deeply, decorating her words with large, red hearts forming a border around the page. I was gratified by her praise, but knew I hadn't earned it. I was aware that I had a long way to go before I was an accomplished teacher. It was almost as if her words were prophetic for me, though; I wanted to be the kind of teacher that left a mark like that on a child.

My second year I changed grade levels, schools, and states, moving north to marry Pat and settle into a rural northern corner of Oregon. But even with all of that change, the teaching was easier the second time around. I understood the processes better—how to plan a field trip, how to plan a unit, how to plan ahead—and my students bene-fited. We accomplished more.

What is hard for me to fathom is that many new teachers quit after just that much teaching. More quit within three years. They move on to another career. Perhaps they begin managing a restaurant or entering data for a giant software firm. They make more money, I'm sure, but if I had done that, I'd have missed Eric, who called me from jail to say he knew I'd tried, but he just couldn't hold it together. I'd have missed spontaneous birthday parties my students have thrown for me, my nomination as Teacher of the Month this year by Krista and Bethany, who sat in the front row of class each day and encouraged me with their attention and respect. I'd have missed the lessons that hung together like powerful adhesive, those Super Teacher moments that feel like a ride on the Concorde must.

In my experience, it isn't the stress that's left the greatest mark, it is the joy. It bubbles to the surface in the middle of a trying lesson or finds you in a chance meeting with a former student. I consider these moments and think of how lucky I am to have work I love. My career in teaching spans five states, eight grade levels, and hundreds of individual children. Former students have sent me birth announcements and emailed from faraway places. This job is like no other. It will bend your heart to the breaking point one day and exhilarate you the next. It has lessons for a lifetime.

But you have to make it past the first few years.

If we'd ended our marriage over an early battle, I'd have missed Pat and the man he has become. We'd have missed the chance to watch our children grow and change, to see them become independent and singular, to watch how our lessons have formed them and us. We'd have missed the fifteenth-anniversary trip to London and Paris, holding hands at the funeral of Pat's mother, and burying our beloved dog Mishka by the light of a lantern on a cold, April evening. We'd have missed the joy of living life fully, side by side.

The tough question is, What happens to so many of us? We enter teaching with the intention of still being in it when our hair has grayed and our hands have wrinkled. We are idealistic; we want to change lives. So many enter marriage without a consideration of divorce, but something happens. Perhaps the negatives, the daily annoyances, and the battle to reinvent the work each year wear us down. When people ask me how Pat and I have stayed close I always say we talk. A lot. About everything. It can be that simple for teachers, I think. We have to work together more. We have to mentor new teachers, listen to them, and I guess, hold hands once in awhile.

This June, two of my colleagues are retiring from teaching. Collectively they have almost sixty years in the profession. We will honor them with dinner, presents, and speeches, but it is small compared with the honor they have brought teaching by hanging in there.

By making it their life's work.

By refusing to give up.

Teaching is such important work, worth doing well. Students count on us every day to help them see who they can be. We need to stick it out through better and worse, through salary freezes and budget cuts, when we're sick of the bureaucracy as well as when we're energized just by being there. My favorite anniversary gift is a bracelet Pat gave me after he sang in my room that day. It says, "Time passes, love stays." In teaching, the time will pass quickly each year, but our words will live on in the heads of our students and continue to teach them, just as they will continue to teach us.

works cited

Anderson, Laurie Halse, Joan Bauer, Judy Blume, Tom Newkirk, and Naomi Shihab Nye. 2001. "Letters to Teachers." *Voices from the Middle,* November. Urbana, IL: National Council of Teachers of English.

Bomer, Randy. 1995. *Time for Meaning: Crafting Literate Lives in Middle and High School.* Portsmouth, NH: Heinemann.

Calkins, Lucy, with Shelley Harwayne. 1991. *Living Between the Lines.* Portsmouth, NH: Heinemann.

Fraser, Jane. 1998. *Teacher to Teacher: A Guidebook for Effective Mentoring.* Portsmouth, NH: Heinemann.

Graves, Donald H. 2001. *The Energy to Teach.* Portsmouth, NH: Heinemann.

Harwayne, Shelley. 2000. *Lifetime Guarantees.* Portsmouth, NH: Heinemann.

Hinton, S.E. 1997. *The Outsiders.* New York: Viking Press.

Hoekstra, Molly. 2002. *am I teaching yet?* Portsmouth, NH: Heinemann.

Keillor, Garrison. *Lake Wobegon.* New York: Viking Press.

King, Stephen. 2000. *On Writing: A Memoir of the Craft.* New York: Scribner.

Kingsolver, Barbara. 2001. *Prodigal Summer.* New York: Harper Perennial.

Lamott, Anne. 1995. *Bird by Bird: Some Instructions on Writing and Life.* Anchor, NY: Anchor.

Miller, Arthur. 1976. *The Crucible.* New York: Penguin.

Murray, Donald M. 1996. *Crafting a Life in Essay, Story, Poem*. Portsmouth, NH: Boynton/Cook.

——. 1999. *Write to Learn*, 6th edition. Orlando: Harcourt Brace.

Rawls, Wilson. 1984. *Where the Red Fern Grows*. Paramus, NJ: Prentice-Hall.

Rief, Linda, and Maureen Barbieri. 1994. *Workshop 6 The Teacher as Writer*. Portsmouth, NH: Heinemann.

Romano, Tom. 1995. *Writing with Passion: Life Stories, Multiple Genres*. Portsmouth, NH: Heinemann.

Routman, Regie. 1996. *Literacy at the Crossroads*. Portsmouth, NH: Heinemann.

Rowling, J. K. 1999. *Harry Potter and the Chamber of Secrets*. New York: Arthur A. Levine Books.

Rule, Rebecca, and Susan Wheeler. 2000. *True Stories: Guides for Writing from Your Life*. Portsmouth, NH: Heinemann.

Sanders, Scott Russell. 1994. *Staying Put*. Boston: Beacon Press.

Steinbeck, John. 1993. *Of Mice and Men*. New York: Penguin.

Stigler, Jame W., and James Hiebert. 1999. *The Teaching Gap*. New York: Free Press.

afterword: interview with Penny Kittle

Donald M. Murray

In my first semester of teaching at the University of New Hampshire in 1963 I was assigned a class in writing for English Teaching majors. I did not know that I was given the class because, with the anti-education snobbery of the time, no one in the department would teach it.

I also taught a class of self-elected creative writers and journalists. I discovered the best writers were the teaching majors. Although the majority of high school English teachers were women, the textbooks they studied were mostly written by men who taught in universities. I even met one who had never been inside a public high school as a student, parent, visitor, or teacher of teachers.

Many of us have encouraged classroom teachers to write their own professional articles and books in which theory is tempered by practice. In the past thirty-five years a whole library of books have been written by classroom teachers who practice what they preach. They write with their students and they publish books that have the authority of a practitioner.

One of the best of these teacher-writers is Penny Kittle. She had an authority in her early writing that revealed that she had extraordinary potential as a writer. Now that potential has been realized in this powerful, practical book that takes the reader into the classroom. In this interview Penny Kittle talks about how, as a mother, wife, and teacher, she found the time to write and what she learned as a published writing teacher.

What surprised you the most about the process of writing a book?

That I could do it . . . one piece at a time. I found it manageable once I worked on a series of short pieces. Before I just couldn't see far enough ahead to envision an entire book. When I started doing short pieces, I started to move.

What ignited the fire, what caused you to attempt a book?

Don Graves. He kept telling me I had to do it. How could I say no? I've believed everything else he's said. He encouraged me with his energy and his excitement. I wanted to write just to hear him laugh.

How did your attitude toward writing change in the process?

I've always thought of writing as work. It became discovery. I started getting excited to write just because I knew I would end up in a different place than when I began. It was still a lot of work, but the payoff was huge.

What specifically did readers do that helped?

They told me what was working. It was so important to hear people say they understood what I was trying to say or show in my work. When readers said, "I love this. Great line," I wanted to get right back to work again. It was also important to hear them say, "I like this, but the transition is weak." Or, "This is almost there . . . I can see where you're trying to go." It helped me zero in on the problems. Some readers gave me great lines and I stole them.

That hindered?

Sometimes I had to follow my own gut. I spent one evening rewriting a lead for a piece because one of my friends said it didn't work the way it was. He really wanted me to begin the piece the way he wanted and I tried to, but I couldn't do it. I think writers each have their own way . . . their own voice or style . . . you have to respect that and suggest without demanding changes, I guess. It was frustrating work because I was trying to mold a piece of mine into something this other writer was trying to say. That can't work.

What discipline did you use to keep going despite lack of faith?

Keep writing crap. One morning I wrote for four hours. I produced one crappy draft. I told my husband, Pat, I hated giving up four hours on a Saturday just to end up with something that wasn't anything. The other thing I did was reread my own work that I liked, when I got frustrated. It made me believe I could write, I just couldn't write today. I had two particularly good coaches who told me to lower my standards until I could write and I followed their advice.

How did you keep writing while teaching, being a mother, and being a wife?

This was the hardest part. I'm a guilt magnet. If my daughter wanted to come and play her flute in my study, I let her. That meant I couldn't think and certainly not write while she did. I was really torn between wanting to spend time with my kids and my husband and needing to find the time to work on this book. I only accomplished this because Pat and the kids were willing to help me. They did the work around the house and let me write. Pat was completely supportive. He delivered breakfast to my study almost every Saturday. He'd sneak in and read the most recent documents to find out what I was writing and then tell me how much he loved my work. Plus, he's a great cook and he's always finding cool projects to do with our kids. I knew they were well cared for when I was preoccupied.

Teaching actually helped me most of the time. I wrote from what I experienced every day at school. And I was compelled to write because of the challenges we continue to face at A. Crosby Kennett Jr./ Sr. High School every day. I work with terrific people. The exhaustion of teaching drained me, but the experiences helped me. And I learned things by writing that I loved to bring back to my classroom. Teaching is energizing, as is writing.

How did your family help or hinder?

They valued this as important work. My ten-year-old daughter and I were seated side by side on a plane trip home from Oregon at Christmas and she saw that I had a draft with me. She asked to read it. She started making notes on it, reading it like a critical editor would. It was fascinating. And it helped.

There were times when I wanted to ship them all off to Mars. Our house has all wood floors, and the doors to my study are glass ones. My kids are loud. We have a dog and two cats. If they had friends over in the afternoon and started playing, I wanted to scream. But this is their house, too, and I tried to be reasonable. My daughter would interrupt me about five times before she stopped some days. And at other times the phone would ring and no one would get it. Stupid things made me crazy. I just had to regroup, rethink, and start again each time. On good writing days, they were easy to ignore. On frustrating ones, they were the perfect excuse to give up.

When did you have to avoid readers?

Early in a draft, especially one that I didn't like yet. I'm impatient when someone reads my work and then tells me exactly what I already know is wrong with it. If there was too much going wrong at once, a poor read might make me give up on it. I needed to let things settle before I sent them out to an audience.

What reader responses did you have to learn to ignore?

General writing advice that can't be applied to every situation. "A lead should grab the reader by the lapels and not let go." Yeah, maybe. Or most of the time. I couldn't make all of mine fit this and when I tried, I left my desk in frustration. I had to trust that I had a story to tell and that it might not fit all of the advice books, but if I was true to the story, it would be worth hearing.

What was the role of your editor?

Lois was this authority in my mind. She's Don [Graves'] editor and I love his work, so I knew she was good. She also edits several other people whose work I admire and use. She was a big gun and I was terrified of her. Her praise was a big deal. The first few times she sent me an encouraging email, I printed it and took it to work with me, reading it over several times during the day to feel sure it was real. She is a cheerleader and she helped me believe in me. She is also great at nailing things that have to change. What she did was encourage me to write and write and write. I got a lot of encouragement to revise and improve on my own. And she's just so nice! We had lunch and I couldn't help but trust her. She's adorable.

How did the writing of the book change your teaching?

I said fewer ridiculous things to my students about writing. Like, "Brainstorm three leads and then choose the best one and go from there." I learned how unique a writer's process is and to encourage my students to trust their own knowledge of their subject enough to write. I started understanding what students were doing when they avoided completing an assignment. I gave my students more time to think and revise. I became much more skillful at rooting out the essential problems in a piece, so my conferences were shorter and more meaningful.

What did your readers or your editor teach you about teaching?

Be positive. Encouragement works; criticism hurts. Be careful with words.

What did you have to keep from showing readers—or showing readers too early?

Titles. They are easy to take shots at and most of mine are uninspired . . . truly awful. A title is just a few words, so you figure anyone can write one. But I can't. At least not the first time.

What did the writing itself teach you?

The moves a writer makes. What to do next. There was also this period I'll call "the zone." When I was in it, writing was just humming along for days at a time. Then if I got knocked out of it, I stopped. Also, that ideas surface all the time and I should carry something with me to write down key ones. It feels like a little lightbulb over my head sometimes. I've got one! Quick . . . give me a pencil.

How important is attitude and how do you now teach attitude?

Self-talk was important. I'd tell myself, "You can do this. Just write what happened and go back and fix it later." I want everything perfect the first time. This is entirely the wrong career for me, because my work is full of errors and I hate it. I don't know how to teach attitude. I told my students to write their own stories and then encouraged them in every way I could.

At what point did you know you were going to finish?

When I wrote "earning my stripes." This piece was fun to write; it made me laugh. I had to keep going after that.

What will you do differently in your next book?

I'll take better notes to help with the writing. One of the easiest pieces to write was "watching Joe" because I had my notes from the classroom observation with me. Writing down exact dialogue is huge because I never get it right if I'm just relying on memory. But truthfully, I can't imagine another book. I'm writing in my head all the time, but I'm just as apprehensive now as I was when I started. Why would anyone want to read what I've written? I'll have to read *Art & Fear* [David Bayles and Ted Orland, Capra Press] again, I think.

What advice do you have for a teacher who wants to write?

Start by writing what you assign for your students to do. Even journal entries. Try completing the short stories or poetry or whatever. I remember writing "ode to Dan" with my ninth graders when we found out Dan Kimball was moving. I couldn't believe how hard it was. It gave me a new appreciation for how much time some of the homework we assign really takes.

What writing tools did you use?

Obviously a computer. I love cut and paste. I use a thesaurus all the time. I read a lot of what other writers have to say about writing. *Crafting a Life* [Murray] was an important book for me. Others by Rebecca Rule and Susan Wheeler [*True Stories: A Guide for Writing from Your Life*], Annie Lamott [*Bird by Bird*], and Stephen King [*On Writing*] were great. I have a journal where I record quotes that make me think.

Did you have a writing place?

I have a room. I believe in Virginia Woolf's assertion that many women did not write in prior centuries because they had nowhere to go. I need this space. There is a couch in the turret that looks out over the woods that surround our house. So I write and print, and then flop on the couch and read and think. Then back to my desk. The only problem is, it is on the first floor of the house, where all the action is. Sometimes it is too noisy. I have my sign from you, "nulla dies sine linea," (never a day without a line) and colored pencils for drawing. I love it here.

Did you have a regular writing time?

Best times have been 4:00 A.M. before school, or 6:30 on a Saturday morning. I need that peace in the house and a large mug of coffee. But the truth is, when I'm humming along on a piece, I can come home after work and work. Lately it has been after dinner for an hour. If it is in my head, I can work at any time. If I'm struggling, I start sleeping in.

How has writing a book affected your reading of a book?

I used to think great writing was all genius. Now I appreciate the work the writer put into getting there. I'm constantly thinking as I read, noticing craft and sentence structure and how big ideas are shown in little scenes. I've always been attentive to word choice, but now even more so. I'm also rereading some stuff, thinking, "Why did I like this so much?" And I'm reading everything I can find from my favorite authors.

What did you learn about anticipating and answering the reader's questions?

They are the voices in my head as I write. I always hear them questioning my thinking, my points, my accuracy. And I find I don't have answers for many of the questions, but they keep me pondering. Audience is always central when you're writing. You have to imagine they're beside you, listening. In this case, I always pictured a teacher, someone working tirelessly to support kids, but feeling misunderstood and maligned by the constant battering in the media. I just wanted to pull up a chair and talk about teaching.